MIKE LUTTRELL
257-0880

TAHOE

ROCK CLIMBING

CHRISTINE JENKEWITZ-MEYTRAS

CHOCKSTONE PRESS

WARNING

This is only a guide book. It is merely a composite of opinions from many sources on the whereabouts and difficulties of various routes. It is not an instructional book on mountaineering technique or a substitute for the user's judgement. Rock climbing is a high risk sport and the user of this book assumes full responsibility for his or her safety.

CONTENTS

vi

Published and distributed by:
CHOCKSTONE PRESS, INC.
526 Franklin Street
Denver, CO 80218
(303) 377-1970

ISBN 0-934641-04-8

FOREWORD

Since the 1960's California's Sierra Nevada has attracted rock climbers from around the world, most of whom have come to climb the famous walls in Yosemite National Park. Meanwhile, the northern California and Nevada climbers who have explored outcrops north of the park have been rewarded with superb rock climbing.

Rock climbers have been plying their craft on the numerous crags in the Lake Tahoe region for about forty years. I've personally spent the last twenty years climbing here, and in my opinion the area has more to offer than most climbers realize.

While the cliffs around Tahoe offer excellent climbing, information about the routes has been sketchy. Local climbers have usually been able to get around this problem but the visiting climber has often left the area feeling somewhat frustrated. Since 1967, various articles, published guidebooks and underground topo guides have appeared; however, none of these have been comprehensive in their coverage of Tahoe climbing. Hundreds of outcrops are located here and much activity has gone unrecorded. Some of the more active climbers have made it clear they oppose a guidebook for the area.

I have long hoped for a guidebook to the entire region. When Christine Jenkewitz-Meytras expressed her interest in editing a new guide I was naturally delighted and supportive. We both agree that a guidebook serves the entire climbing community. It is my pleasure to endorse her work and commend her effort.

GENE DRAKE

PREFACE

The last rock climbing guide to the Tahoe region was published in 1980 by Rick Sumner. That guidebook has been out of print for three years, and since that time numerous new routes have been done. The purpose of this new guide is to provide a catalog of information to the climber willing to discover the wealth of fine climbing in the Tahoe area. A new feature in this book is the addition of a major climbing area on the North Shore of Lake Tahoe, Donner Summit, which was not included in previous guides.

A number of climbs on lesser cliffs and rocks have been deliberately excluded from this book. The crags that require a long or strenuous approach and have climbs that are not particularly notable are still mentioned but not in any great detail — many of these routes have not seen a second ascent. If the reader is interested in finding out more about them, he or she can ask the local climbers or consult the local mountaineering shop or guide service.

Most of the routes in this guide are described by topo. This graphic presentation of the cliffs and their climbs is the most precise and convenient means of route description. A few of the routes are still given written descriptions, either because detailed information was unavailable or it was too poor to use in topos. There will, of course, be some errors because perceptions differ and memories alter with time. Climbers are encouraged to write to the author in care of Chockstone Press, 526 Franklin Street, Denver, Colorado 80218.

I gratefully acknowledge the help and information provided by many local climbers. Particular thanks are due to David Babich, Gene Drake, Karl Jenkewitz, Alan Miller, Steve Miller, George Connor, and Jay Smith. I would also like to thank Harvey Overland and Bill Serniuk for the use of their photographs, as credited.

I would like to apologize to those climbers who may feel offended because some of their routes are not included, or because their favorite area is not described in detail, but there were choices to be made and ultimately those decisions had to be mine. The guidebook editor's position can be an awkward one; reactions to such an undertaking run the gamut from full-bore enthusiasm to outright hostility, and it is never possible to please everyone. It is my feeling that a topo guide to the Tahoe area was long overdue and that such a guide is a positive addition to the climbing experience, and I hope that you will enjoy my work and find it useful.

In closing, I would like to add that this guidebook was not written to please local climbers or to honor their climbing prowess, but to help the visitor explore this beautiful climbing area by making available accurate information about the many great climbs of the Tahoe Basin.

Good climbing to all of you!

Let us probe the silent places,
Let us seek what luck betide us,
Let us journey to a lonely land I know,
There's a whisper on the night wind,
There's a star agleam to guide us,
And the wild is calling, calling . . . let us go.

HENRY DAVID THOREAU

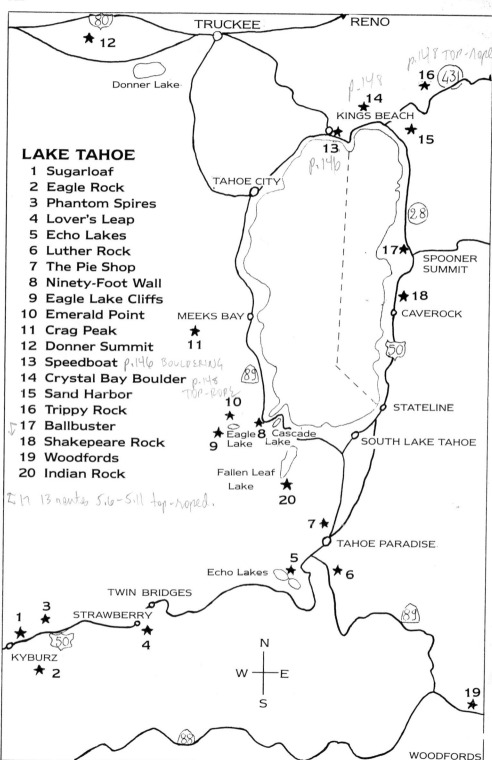

LAKE TAHOE

1 Sugarloaf
2 Eagle Rock
3 Phantom Spires
4 Lover's Leap
5 Echo Lakes
6 Luther Rock
7 The Pie Shop
8 Ninety-Foot Wall
9 Eagle Lake Cliffs
10 Emerald Point
11 Crag Peak
12 Donner Summit
13 Speedboat p.146 BOULDERING
14 Crystal Bay Boulder p.148 TOP-ROPE
15 Sand Harbor
16 Trippy Rock
17 Ballbuster
18 Shakepeare Rock
19 Woodfords
20 Indian Rock

In 13 routes 5.6 - 5.11 top-roped.

INTRODUCTION

The rock formations described in this book lie near Lake Tahoe, a clear, pristine and large lake — the deepest high altitude freshwater lake in North America — nestled high in the Sierra Nevada of California about 200 miles due east of San Francisco. There are few places in the world that offer Tahoe's radically different atmospheres. Excellent rock in a gorgeous alpine environment sits next to the inexpensive food and lodging provided by the resort towns around the lake. But more than that, the wilderness climbing contrasts starkly with the wild night life and glittery entertainment of the throbbing gambling town of South Lake Tahoe.

Lake Tahoe is bordered on the west and east by mountains made of granitic and metamorphic rock. Volcanic rock is found in the northern sections. Most of the climbing crags are of a granite called granodiorite. With few exceptions the rock on the west side of the lake tends to be solid and compact while that on the east tends to be more crumbly. In addition to the many crags located near the lake, this book also describes the major cliffs of Lover's Leap, 19 miles from the "Y" in South Shore, and Donner Summit, situated 15 miles north of Tahoe City.

The rock on all these crags varies widely in texture, from the smooth fine granite of Donner Summit or Eagle Lake Buttress to the coarse rough stone of the Pie Shop, from the crack systems of Eagle Lake Cliffs to the dike-striped Lover's Leap and the knobby faces of Phantom Spires. Frequently the character of the climb changes from pitch to pitch, and this textural variety offers combination climbs which are unique to the Tahoe region. What is constant is great climbing.

Lake Tahoe is within a three or four hour drive of the San Francisco area, two hours from Sacramento, and one hour from Reno, Nevada. The town of Truckee, located on the north shore of the lake, is but 45 minutes east of Sacramento and west of Reno via Interstate 80. The town is about an hour's drive up either side of the lake from the city of South Lake Tahoe.

Transportation to and from the area is easy. Lake Tahoe is served by two major highways, Interstate 80 on the north and U.S. Highway 50 on the south. Other, smaller state roads reach into the basin, as well. South Lake Tahoe has a small airport that is open all year and is served by at least one public airline, AirCal. The national bus lines come to the lake, as well as casino-sponsored bus transportation from the major cities nearby. For three seasons of the year weather is not a problem, but the lake is in a high mountain environment and sudden winter storms can cause road and airport closures.

WEATHER

The weather in the Tahoe region is generally mild. Summer temperatures at lake level seldom exceed the seventies, and there are few thunderstorms. The winters are not rigorous but are characterised by quick wet storms followed by periods of excellent and warm weather. Depending on the snow cover, it is possible to climb all year on southern exposures or at the lower elevations like Sugarloaf, Phantom Spires, or Woodfords's Canyon.

AREA	ELEVATION	CLIMBING SEASON
Sugarloaf	4400'	All year
Phantom Spires	5200-5900'	All year
Lover's Leap	6944'	April-November
Hogsback	6200'	April-November
Echo Lakes	7700-8363'	May-November
The Pie Shop	6700'	All year
Indian Rock	8560'	May November
Ninety-Foot Wall	6700'	April-November
Eagle Lake Cliffs	7200-8640'	May-November
Eagle Lake Buttress		
Emerald Point	9195'	April-November
Crag Peak	9054'	June-November
Donner Summit	7000'	May-October
East Shore areas	6300-7100'	March-November
Luther Rock	6800'	April-November
Woodford's Canyon	5500'	All year

Highway 40 is closed from November to April

WHERE TO STAY

Camping near Tahoe is pleasant and easy. In the North Shore area alone are six National Forest campgrounds. Many private campgrounds are scattered throughout the lake basin, providing good sites and amenities for reasonable fees. Free camping is available both at Lover's Leap and at the top of Donner Summit. (In the latter area the Sheriff's Department generally enforces a three day limit.) Be aware that most of the groundwater in the Tahoe Basin is contaminated with Giardia. It is best to treat all water obtained from streams or lakes. The only exception to this is the small perennial spring at the top of Lover's Leap. Inexpensive and plentiful meals are available in the casinos, and the many local restaurants and stores provide a diverse selection of good food.

CLIMBING HISTORY

Climbing in the Lake Tahoe area has become increasingly popular in the last 15 years. The many fine crags have seen much activity and have provided routes of a very high standard.   Little is known of the very early climbing days in the Tahoe basin and on the crags along Highway 50 on the west side of the mountains. Lover's Leap and the Sugarloaf were probably the first cliffs to see any climbing activity, and it is said that at this early time the climbers were so few that the parties would go out of their way to meet each other. Climbing at Donner Summit started with mountaineer/ climbers like John Orangehal, from Reno, Nevada. They used the area to practice aid climbing and top roping.

In the late sixties, **The Line** on Lover's Leap, which was then an aid route, was climbed free by Tom Higgins and Frank Sarnquist; it was a psychological opening for hard free climbing. Soon after, TM Herbert and Bruce Cooke established the strenuous **TM's Deviation** (5.9+) at the Sugarloaf. Lover's Leap saw much activity in 1969, when eleven new routes and free ascents were accomplished, with Steve Roper's guide-like write-up in the 1967 *Ascent* certainly having something to do with this surge of exploration. The most spectacular ascent of this year was probably Jeff Lowe's first and solo ascent of **The Hourglass Wall**, 5.9, climbed in April under winter conditions. **The Direct Start of Surrealistic Pillar**, at 5.10 the hardest route established at Lover's Leap until 1972, was also climbed during this year.

Jim Orey contributed enormously to the climbing development of the Tahoe area in the early seventies, and because of his efforts, climbing at the Sugarloaf became more advanced. With Gene Drake he climbed **Vanishing Point** (5.10) at Lover's Leap in 1972. It was the hardest jam crack in all the Tahoe area in this year. Ken Volz ascended **Separated Reality** (5.8) and **Off the Wall**, an aid route. While by 1972 only two 5.10 routes existed in the entire region, Eric Beck published a small guide to Tahoe, describing mostly Donner Summit, and shortly after, the local climbers from Truckee, the Tahoe City area and Reno started to climb there intensively. By the late seventies many 5.10 routes had been climbed there.

The three most classic lines on Eagle Lake Buttress, **A Line**, **Monkey Business**, and **Orange Sunshine**, were climbed in 1974 by Rick Sumner, John Taylor and Bill Todd. The climbing at Echo Lakes was significant with Bill Todd's ascents of **EB's Wall** (5.10b), rival to **East Corner** in difficulty, and the first free ascent of **Jam Session** (5.10a).

INTRODUCTION

In the mid seventies free soloing came into popularity. The movement was started by Rick Sumner and followed by Bill Todd and Steve Miller, and the first climbs were recorded at Luther Rock. In 1976 the Sugarloaf saw the first 5.11 lead in the Tahoe area, on **Taurus,** and at Lover's Leap the local climbers were very active: Greg Dexter, Steve Miller, Paul Crawford, Jay Smith, Bill Todd and Rick Sumner. Fifteen new routes, variations and free ascents were climbed on Lover's Leap alone in 1977. The competition was strong. Jay Smith was certainly the most successful climber; with Richard Harrison, Smith created **Purple Haze** (5.10d), the hardest route of the time at the Leap.

At the Sugarloaf, Mark Hudon and Max Jones pushed the standards higher with the first free ascent of the initial arch of **Hooker's Haven** (5.12), in 1978, and Mark Hudon free soloed the 5.11b **Taurus. Mainline** (5.11c), at Lover's Leap, was freed by John Bachar and Ron Kauk in 1978, and Tony Yaniro directed his attention to the east face of Dear John Buttress with several routes ranging from 5.11c to 5.11d. In 1979, the Sugarloaf became one of the hardest climbing areas in the country with the first 5.13 ever climbed by Yaniro: **Grand Illusion.** Several routes in the 5.11 and 5.12 realm were also climbed by Mark Hudon, Max Jones and Tony Yaniro. Echo Lakes and Eagle Lake Cliffs received much attention, and some beautiful routes were climbed. **Kangaroo** (5.10b), on Flagpole Peak, was climbed by Jim Orey, Jon Bowlin and Jim Day, and **Space Walk** (5.11d), on Eagle Lake Cliff, was led by Rick Sumner and Rick Cashner.

In the early eighties, the local climbers, mostly Paul Crawford, Jay Smith and Karl McConachie were very active in the Tahoe area, starting with Sugarloaf and the Phantom Spires (where Sacramento climbers like George Connor and David Babich had already established numerous new routes. The competition is strong and the remaining possibilities for new routes scarce. Many climbs in the 5.12 + realm have been done in the last few years, and Lover's Leap is now a crag crowded with routes. Donner Summit now boasts more 5.12 routes than in the entire Tahoe region, and because of the quality, if not the length of these climbs, Donner has seen a great surge in popularity.

HOW TO USE THIS GUIDE

This guidebook is of selected climbs compiled from west to east in the order one would encounter each area while driving up Highway 50 from Placerville to South Lake Tahoe, to the junction of Highway 89 North. This junction is referred to locally as the "Y". From the "Y" the route goes up the west shore of the lake via 89, and continues clockwise around the lake shore to return to the "Y," and then out Highway 89 South over Luther Pass and down in to Woodford's Canyon. The sections on Lesser Rocks and Crags, Top Roping areas, and Bouldering follow the same sequence, as does the final chapter on Tahoe ice climbing.

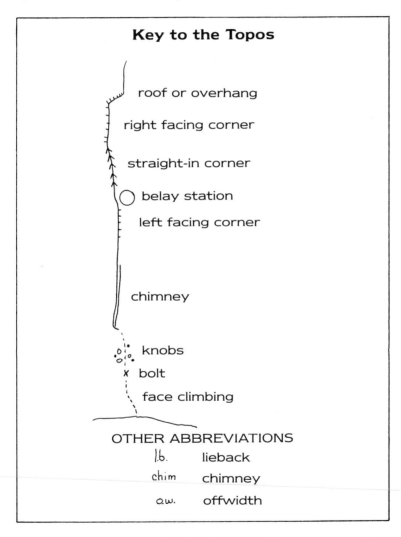

Key to the Topos

roof or overhang

right facing corner

straight-in corner

belay station

left facing corner

chimney

knobs

bolt

face climbing

OTHER ABBREVIATIONS

l.b.	lieback
chim	chimney
o.w.	offwidth

The rating system used in this book is the standard Yosemite Decimal System. "Third" and "Fourth"-class refers to easy scrambling over increasingly hazardous terrain, and the fifth class climbing is rated in levels of difficulty from 5.1 to the current extreme of 5.13c. I have added the "R" and "X" notations to the topos, where "R"indicates poor protection or a long runout, and "X" indicates the possibility of a very serious or fatal fall. (**Note that the Donner Summit topos do not include these notations.**) As with all the route descriptions found in this book, these severity ratings are subjective and assume that all users of this guide are competent in the use of protection devices. Simply because a route does not have a seriousness rating does not imply that protection is readily available. Once on the rock, routefinding and responsibility for your safety is strictly yours. This book is only a guide to the routes; it is not a substitute for sound mountaineering judgement.

One of the nicer things about climbing in the Tahoe area is that the local climbers, though they climb at a very high standard, do not scream too much about the inconsistency of climbing ethics, and it is possible to enjoy one's own climbing experience without a watchdog criticising your methods . . . However, this relaxed attitude does imply a respect for the current standard ethic of climbing clean and in good style, thus ensuring that the routes suffer only from the weather.

The topos may give protection needs beyond the usual free climbing rack that includes R.P.'s, Rocks and some Friends. Simply because the topo information is lacking in these notations does not mean, however, that such special protection needs are never required; this is only a guide, and the climber's best (and ultimate) protection lies with his/her judgement.

RECOMMENDED CLIMBS
Traveller Buttress (5.7 face – lower pitch) Lover's Leap
Corrugation Corner (5.7 face) Lover's Leap
Bear's Reach (5.7 face) Lover's Leap
Surrealistic Pillar Regular (5.7 face) Lover's Leap
Over Easy (5.7 face) Phantom Spires
Pie in the Sky (5.7 face) The Pie Shop
The Groove (5.8 face) Lover's Leap
Wave Rider (5.8 face) Lover's Leap
Jellyroll Arch (5.8 face) Donner Summit
Eagle Buttress, right (5.9 face) Lover's Leap
Fear No Evil (5.9 face) Lover's Leap
Fantasia (5.9 face) Lover's Leap
Short Cake (5.9 face) Donner Summit
B.T. Express (5.9 face) The Pie Shop
Leapin' Lizards (5.9 face) Echo Lakes
Super Slab (5.10a face) Donner Summit
Empty Sky (5.10a face) Donner Summit
Captain Coconuts (5.10a face) Lover's Leap
Ozzie (5.10a face) Lover's Leap
Surrealistic Pillar Direct (5.10a face) Lover's Leap
Jack of Hearts (5.10a face) Donner Summit
True Grip (5.10b face) The Pie Shop

Wind (5.10b face) The Pie Shop
Off the Wall (5.10b face) Eagle Creek Canyon
Kangaroo (5.10b face) Echo Lakes
E.B.'s Wall (5.10b face) Echo Lakes
Bolee Gold (5.10c face) Sugarloaf
Candyland (5.10c face) Phantom Spires
101 Dalmations (5.10c face) Phantom Spires
Epitaph (5.10c face) Lover's Leap
Goldilocks (5.10d face) Donner Summit
Char Broiled (5.10d face) Phantom Spires
Bolt Run (5.10d face) Donner Summit
Under The Big Top (5.10d face) Lover's Leap
Dancin' Feet (5.10d face) Lover's Leap
East Corner (5.10d face) Lover's Leap
Out to Lunge (5.10d face) Lover's Leap
Easier Said Than Done (5.10d face) Lover's Leap
Glaze-Her-Face (5.11a A1 face) Lover's Leap
Boothill (5.11a face) Lover's Leap
Fingerlicker (5.11a face) Donner Summit
Wipeout (5.11a face) The Pie Shop
Wet Dreams var. (5.11a face) Phantom Spires
The Man Who Fell to Earth (5.11b face) Sugarloaf
Sizzler (5.11b face) Phantom Spires
If I Had a Hammer (5.11b face) Echo Lakes
More Madness (5.11b face and thin) Lover's Leap

Devaluation (5.7 lieback) Donner Summit
Ambrosia (5.7 lieback) The Pie Shop
Rated X (5.8-9 lieback) Donner Summit
Touch and Go (5.9 lieback) Donner Summit
Farley (5.9 lieback) Sugarloaf
Pony Express (5.9 lieback) Sugarloaf
Bourbon Street (5.10a lieback) Donner Summit
Tombstone Terror (5.10c lieback) Lover's Leap
Seams to Me (5.10c lieback) Eagle Creek Canyon
Karl's Gym (5.10d lieback) Donner Summit
Steppin' Stone (5.11a undercling) Phantom Spires
Manic Depression (5.11c lieback) Donner Summit
Der Führer (5.11d tr lieback) Eagle Creek Canyon
Hooker's Haven (5.12a lieback) Sugarloaf

Summer Breeze (5.8 thin) Echo Lakes
Lean and Mean (5.9 thin) Phantom Spires
Scimitar (5.9 thin) Lover's Leap
The Line (5.9 thin) Lover's Leap
Pitchfork (5.8-5.10a thin) Echo Lakes
Fear of Flying (5.9/5.10b thin) Phantom Spires

Hospital Corner (5.10a thin) Lover's Leap
Magnum Force (5.10b thin) Lover's Leap
True Grip (5.10b thin) The Pie Shop
End of the Line (5.10b thin) Lover's Leap
Robert's Crack var. (5.10c thin) Phantom Spires
Roofer Madness (5.10c thin) Lover's Leap
Hemorrhoids in Flight (5.10d thin) Lover's Leap
Thrust is a Must (5.10d thin) Eagle Creek Canyon
Fracture (5.10d thin) Sugarloaf
Purple Haze (5.10d thin) Lover's Leap
K.E. Cracks (5.11 thin) Phantom Spires
Black Pyre (5.11a thin) Lover's Leap
The Cross Town Traffic var. (5.11a thin) Lover's Leap
The Hourglass (5.11a thin) Lover's Leap
More Madness (5.11b thin) Lover's Leap
Taurus (5.11b thin) Sugarloaf
Stoney End (5.11c thin) Lover's Leap
Space Walk (5.11c/d thin) Eagle Creek Canyon
North Face Lizard Head (5.11c tr thin) Phantom Spires
Stone Cold Crazy (5.12c thin) Lover's Leap
The Silly Willy Crack (5.12c thin) Lover's Leap
Grand Illusion (5.13c thin) Sugarloaf

Crepes Corner (5.7 hand) The Pie Shop
Bookmark (5.7 hand) Lover's Leap
Hands Masseuse (5.8 hand) The Pie Shop
The Slot (5.8 hand) The Pie Shop
Jugs Revisited (5.9 hand) Phantom Spires
Nova Express (5.9 hand) Donner Summit
Space Truckin' (5.10a hand) Eagle Creek Canyon
Firecracker (5.10b hand) Donner Summit
Vanishing Point (5.10b lieback/hand) Lover's Leap
Black Opal (5.10c hand) Lover's Leap
Main Line (5.11c thin hand) Lover's Leap
Eyore's Enigma (5.10a offwidth/chimney) Lover's Leap
Third Stone From the Sun (5.10c fist) Lover's Leap
God of Thunder (5.11+ fist/face) Lover's Leap

Composure (5.6 combo) Donner Summit
Deception (5.6 combo) Lover's Leap
East Wall (5.6 combo) Lover's Leap
Eleventh Grade (5.8 combo) Donner Summit
Haystack (5.8) Lover's Leap
Black September (5.9) Donner Summit
Peter Principle (5.10a) Donner Summit
Teacher's Pet (5.10b combo) Donner Summit
Farewell to Arms (5.10b) Donner Summit

SUGARLOAF

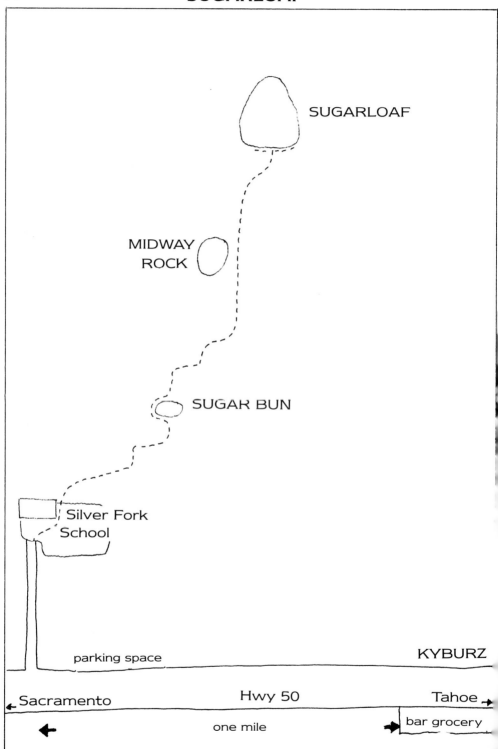

SUGARLOAF

MIDWAY
ROCK

SUGAR BUN

Silver Fork
School

parking space

KYBURZ

Sacramento

Hwy 50

Tahoe

one mile

bar grocery

SUGARLOAF

Thirty miles west of South Lake Tahoe on Highway 50 is the little town of Kyburz. On the hillside to the north rises the 400 foot crag of Sugarloaf. The granite at Sugarloaf is good but different from that found in the Tahoe Basin or at Lover's Leap. The routes follow well-formed crack and chimney systems, between which are steep slabs that provide beautiful face and friction climbing. Located in the lower Sierra, at 4900 feet, Sugarloaf offers year round climbing. It is here that Tony Yaniro put up **Grand Illusion,** the first climb to be rated 5.13.

Park your car on the side of Highway 50, off the road, near the private road that leads to Silver Fork school. Do not park on this private road — there have been problems with the people who live along it. Walk up toward the school and find the trail that starts to the right of the schoolyard. Follow this trail past big boulders and up a steep and sandy slope to the base of the south face of Sugarloaf. The approach takes 30-40 minutes and the section above the boulders can be strenuous (especially in hot weather).

Sugarloaf has three distinct summits, the middle one being the highest. To descend from any of the routes ending on the middle or north summit, walk north along the top to a tree that enables one to descend a short wall. A gully then leads north to the ground via easy class 3.

EASIER ROUTES TEND TO BE CHIMNEYS

SUGARBUN

Sugarbun is the most popular of the lesser rocks below Sugarloaf. It is located about 100 yards above the Silver Fork schoolyard and its top is visible from there. Sugarbun has no easy side. To get down, make a 60 foot rappel from a tiny tree down the sloping north side.

Fingerlock 70', 5.10b   pro: to 2", mainly small
An oak tree grows beside a long thin crack on the southwest face. Use the tree to bypass a bulge, then jam and lieback to the top.

Make That Move Right Now, Baby 5.10c   pro: 10 quick draws
Start 50 feet right of **Fingerlock,** on top of a boulder. 5.10 moves are made before the crux, which surmounts a three foot roof. Bolts protect face climbing up an arête that leads to the top.

Dirty Dog 60', 5.10c   pro: to 1"
This is an obscure face climb that goes directly up the rappel route on the mossy north face. Two bolts protect the climb.

Mad Dog 100', 5.10c   pro: to 1"
Follow a thin diagonal crack high on the face past **Flytrap's** chimney.

Flytrap 100', 5.7   pro: to 2"
This is the most prominent feature on the north face: a huge flake hiding a chimney. At the top of the flake, climb past a bolt, then traverse right to the rappel tree.

East Corner 100', 5.9   pro: to 4"
Climb a strenuous jam/lieback found in a corner on the east face. The difficulty eases after 30 feet. **Flytrap** is reached at the top of the huge flake.

MIDWAY ROCK

Midway Rock is located halfway between Sugarbun and Sugarloaf.
It is a huge rock split by a flared overhanging slot.

A Flight Deck 5.11d
B Self Abuse 5.10b
C Diagonal 5.9   **Undercling** 5.8

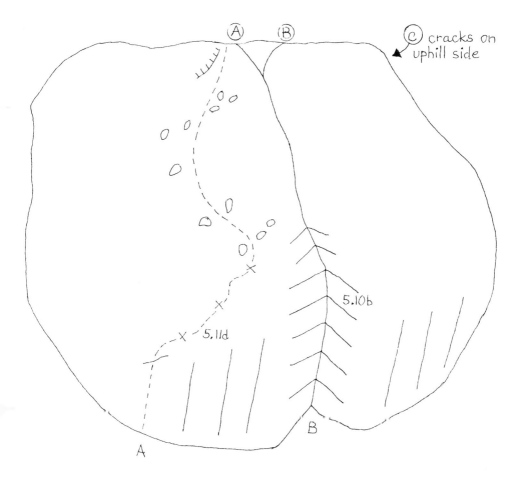

Several routes have been done on the other boulders, ranging up
to 5.11.

SUGARLOAF – East Side

A Farley 5.9
B Taurus 5.11b
C The Fracture 5.10d
D East Chimney 5.7

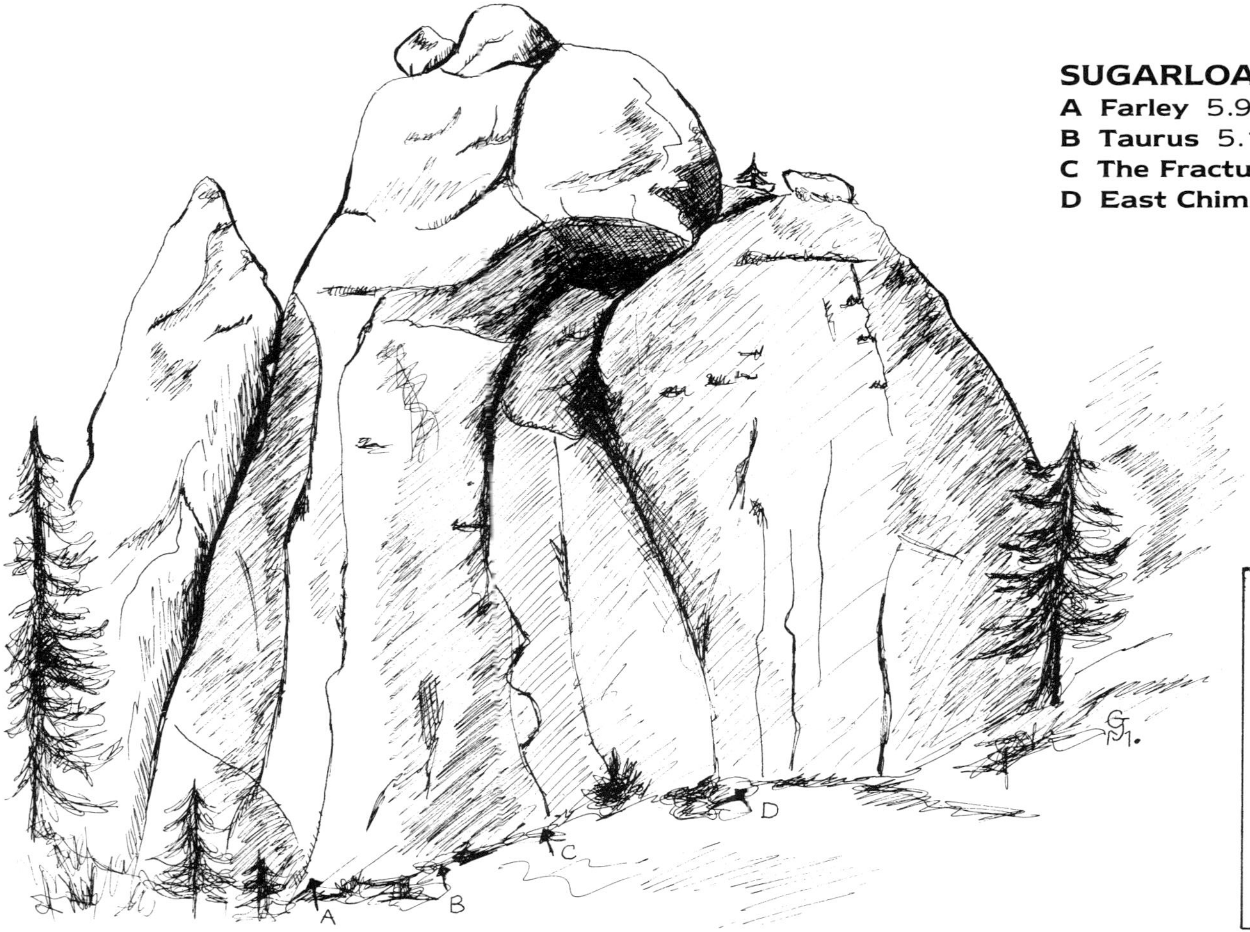

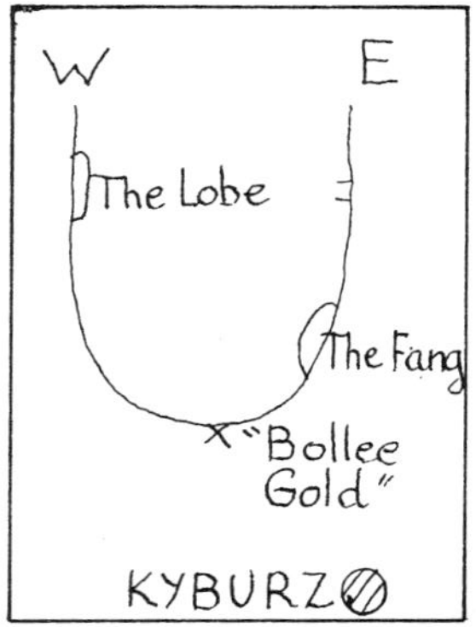

The Lobe

The Fang

X "Bollee Gold"

KYBURZ

W
E

SUGARLOAF – West Side

A **The Podium** 5.9
B **Pony Express** 5.9
C **West Chimney** 5.8
D **Fat Merchant's Crack** 5.10
E **Hooker's Haven** 5.12

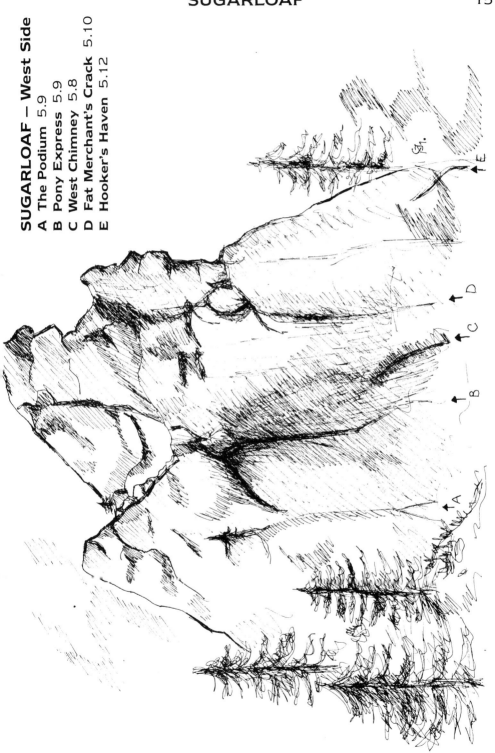

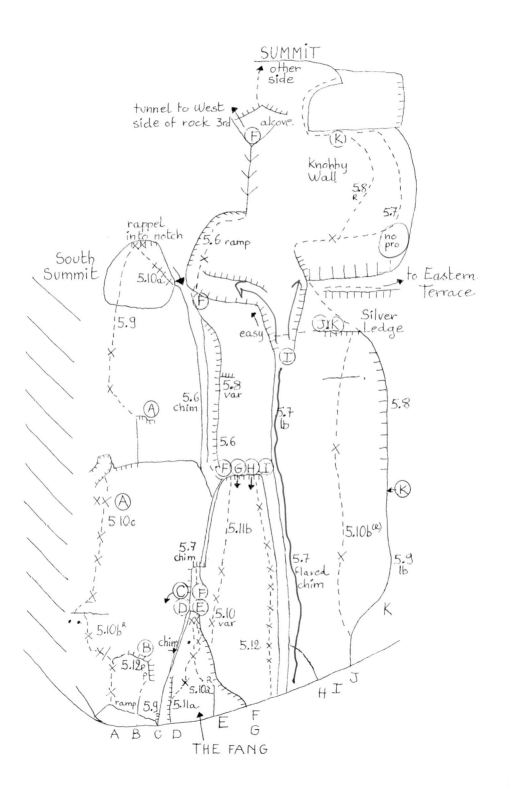

SUMMIT
other side
tunnel to West side of rock 3rd alcove.
Ⓕ
Ⓚ
Knobby Wall
5.8 R
5.7
rappel into notch
5.6 ramp
no pro
South Summit
5.10a
Ⓕ
to Eastern Terrace
5.9
easy
Ⓙ Ⓚ
Silver Ledge
Ⓐ
5.6 chim
5.8 var
Ⓘ
5.7 lb
5.6
5.8
Ⓕ Ⓖ Ⓗ Ⓘ
Ⓚ
XX Ⓐ
5 10c
5.11b
5.10b (R)
5.7 chim
5.7 flared chim
5.9 lb
Ⓒ Ⓕ
Ⓓ Ⓔ
5.10 var
K
5.10b R
Ⓑ chim
5.12
5.12 p E
5.10a R
H I J
ramp 5.9 5.11a
A B C D   E   F
                        G
THE FANG

SUGARLOAF — South Face

A Bolee Gold 5.10c pro: to #7 hex
B Hooker's Haven 5.12a
C The Fang, left side 5.9 pro: to 2"
D Talking Heads 5.11a
E Stone 5.10a R pro: to 2"
F Harding's Chimney 5.7 pro: to 3"
G Gallows Pole 5.11b
H Beast of Burden 5.12
I Scheister 5.7 pro: to 3"
J Tapestry 5.10b R pro: to 1 ½", slings
K Farley 5.9 pro: to 3", mainly larger

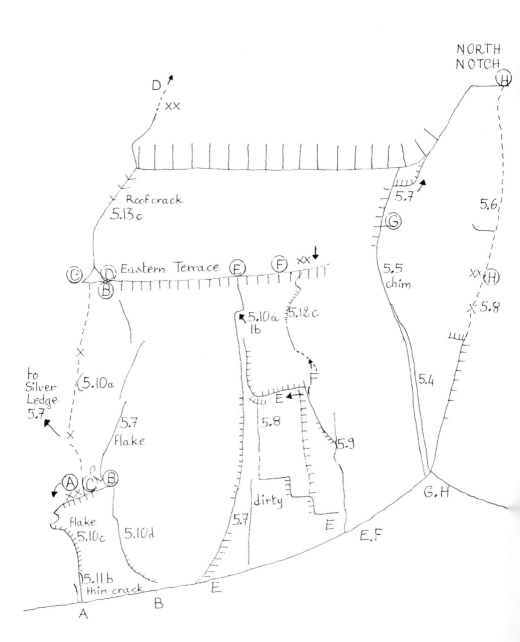

SUGARLOAF — East Face

A Taurus 5.11b pro: to 2½", mainly medium
B The Fracture 5.10d pro: to 1½", mainly thin
C Lady Luck 5.10a
D Grand Illusion 5.13c pro: thin
E Dominion 5.10a pro: to 3"
F Captain Fingers 5.12c pro: to 1½", mainly thin
G East Chimney 5.7 pro: to 3"
H Lurch 5.8 pro: to 2", slings for knobs

Lost in the Fog 400', 5.9 A2 pro: small and medium sizes of chocks, a knifeblade, bathooks and skyhooks
Ascend the blank wall twenty feet left of **Taurus.** Bolts protect this climb. Past the third bolt, climb free (5.9) to a ledge high above on the right. Follow the cracks and chimneys above to Silver Ledge. Continue via **Farley.**

Hanging Jugs 185', 5.8 protection up to 3"
Seventy feet uphill of **East Chimney,** start the climb on a terrace, below a wide crack. Climb the crack to its top. Face climbing next to a thin crack leads to a long and narrow belay ledge. Walk left and ascend a short knobby wall to the top.

Scorpio 130', 5.7 protection up to 2½"
Uphill from **Hanging Jugs** is a left facing and leaning arch. From the top of the arch, face climb on slick holds to the final jam crack.

SUGARLOAF – West Face
A Hyperspace 5.10b pro: to 1½", mainly thin
B Trumpled Under Foot 5.10a R
C Back in Black 5.11d
D The Man Who Fell to Earth 5.11b pro: to 3½"
E The Podium 5.8 pro: to 3½"
F Pony Express 5.9 pro: to 3½"
G Cry Mary 5.12a top rope
H West Chimney 5.8 pro: to 3"
I TM's Deviation 5.9 pro: to 3½"
J Hard Right 5.10c pro: to 2"

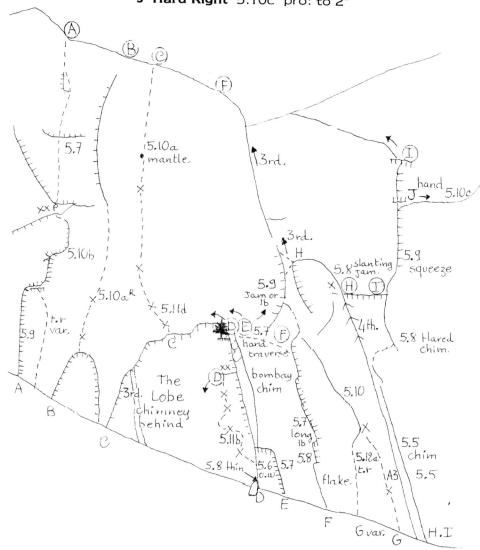

SUGARLOAF — Southwest Face

A Grand Delusion 5.12

B Fat Merchant's Crack
   5.10a   pro: to 5"

C Blindfaith 5.9 variation

D The Ghost in the Machine
   5.12a pro: to 3", many
   slings

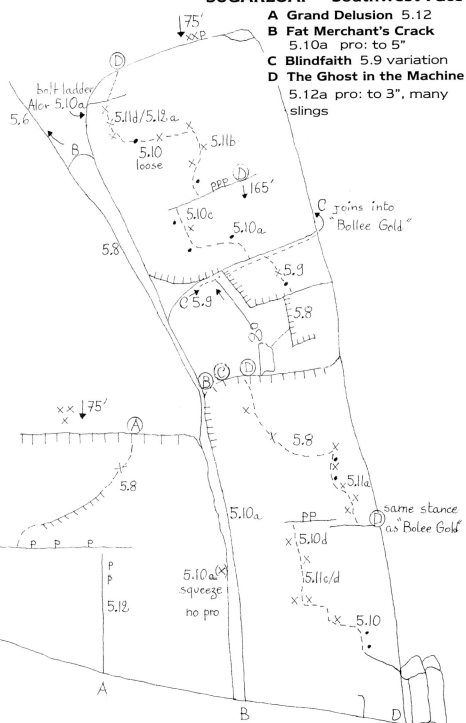

LOST JOHN

FLATHEAD

HELP ME ROCK

UPPER SPIRE
(Grand Pappy)

LIZARD
HEAD

ONE WAY   CLAM ROCK

HAM & EGGS   MIDDLE SPIRE

UNCLE MAX

TWIN OWLS

MIDWAY ROCK

LOWER SPIRE GROUP

PHANTOM WALL

GORILLA
ROCK

ALCOVE

ARMADILLO

HOLIDAY
ROCK

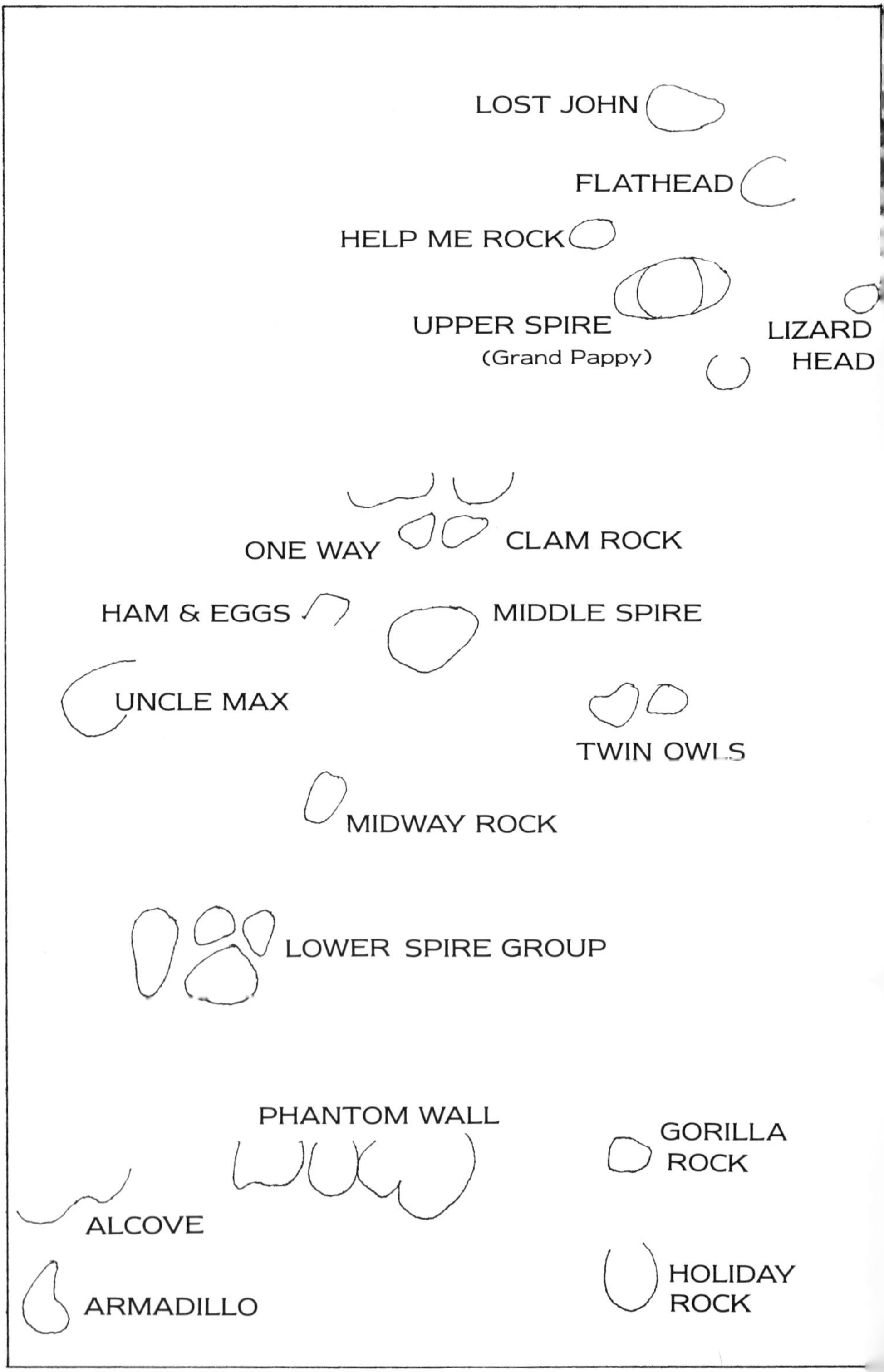

PHANTOM SPIRES

These three spires rise from a burned forest high on the hillside to the north of Highway 50, three miles east of the town of Kyburz. They can be seen from several places along the road, rising in a row toward the northwest. The granite is excellent and so are the routes; the south facing hillside keeps them in the sun, and they afford panoramic views of the American River Canyon and the western foothills. Most of the climbs are on the imaginatively named Lower, Middle, and Upper Spires, but there are numerous other outcrops and smaller formations scattered about, upon which can be found one and two pitch climbs as well as top rope problems, ranging from 5.9 to 5.10c.

To find the Spires, drive east on Highway 50 for three miles past Kyburz. Turn left onto a paved road marked "Wright's Lake." Once in the burn area, about a mile up the road, the Spires come into view directly to the west. At about the same level as Middle Spire, a dirt logging road branches off to the left. Drive along this road as far as you can, then traverse westward on boulders and talus to the Spires.

LOWER SPIRE

Lower Spire is the lowest of the three and stands at the southern end of a cluster of rock. To descend from all the routes, rappel down the northwest face (70 feet).

MIDDLE SPIRE

This spire is up and to the northwest of Lower Spire. The north and west faces are clean and steep. The east face is cut by a large ledge. Descend the east face via a short rappel from bolts.

UPPER SPIRE

This is by far the largest of the three spires; its east face rises 300 feet from the ground and its west face 150 feet. The summit pinnacle is flanked on the north and south by buttresses. The tops of these buttresses form the Lower Platform (south) and the Upper Platform (north). To descend from routes ending on the Lower Platform either rappel to the west from bolts (a doubled 165-foot rope will reach) or climb to the summit via a bolt ladder and an A3 crack. To descend from the summit or the Upper Platform, down climb (4th class) to an oak tree on the west face and rappel 70 feet to the ground.

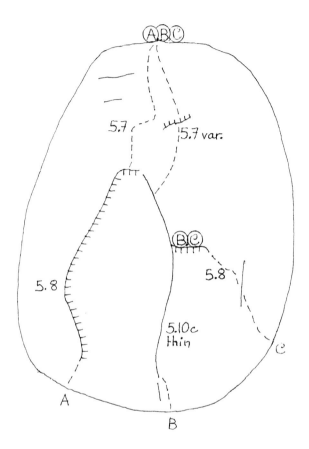

UNCLE MAX — South Side
A The Clown 5.8
B Mean Moe 5.10c
C Coquett 5.8

Descent: down climb off the back side

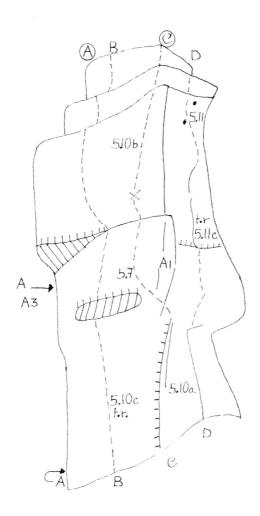

LIZARD HEAD — East Side

A **South Face** A3
B **East Face** 5.10c top rope
C **East Arête** 5.10a A1
D **North Face** 5.11c top rope

Descent: rappel

Desperado
Roof

East Face Route

Steppin'
Stone

Burnt
Offerings

UPPER PHANTOM SPIRE

photo: Christine Jenkewitz-Meytras

UPPER PHANTOM SPIRE — Northeast Side

A Burnt Offerings 5.10d pro: RP's, wires, Friends
B Steppin' Stone 5.11a pro: to 3"
C East Face Route 5.9 pro: to 3"
D Desperado Roof variation
  5.10b pro: to 3"

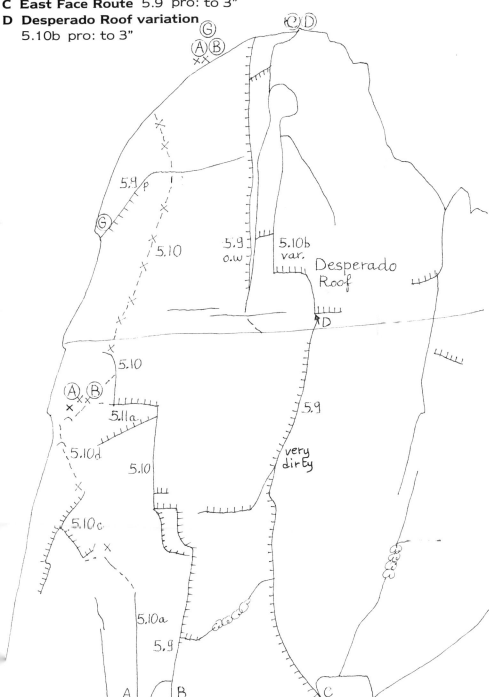

UPPER PHANTOM SPIRE — East Side
A Robert's Crack 5.10d R — 5.10c var. pro: to 2½"
B T Bone 5.10d
C Price-Smith Route 5.10d
D Jugs Revisited 5.9 pro: to 1½"
E Ginger Bread 5.7 pro: to 3"
F Fear of Flying 5.9 variation: 5.10b
G Necklace Traverse 5.10d pro: to 3"
H Burnt Offerings 5.10d pro: RP's, wires, Friends
I Steppin' Stone 5.11a pro: to 3"   photo: Bill Serniuk

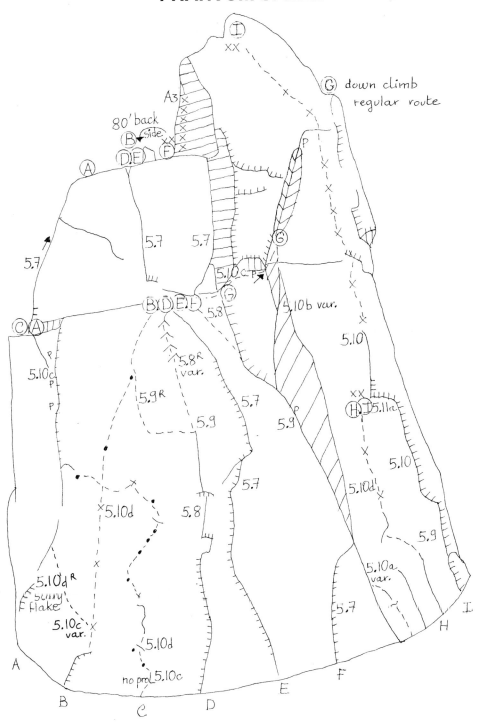

UPPER PHANTOM SPIRE — West Side

A Up for Grabs 5.8
B Sizzler 5.11b
   pro: wires, RP's,
   micro Friends
C The Go Man 5.9
D Lil' Luke 5.9

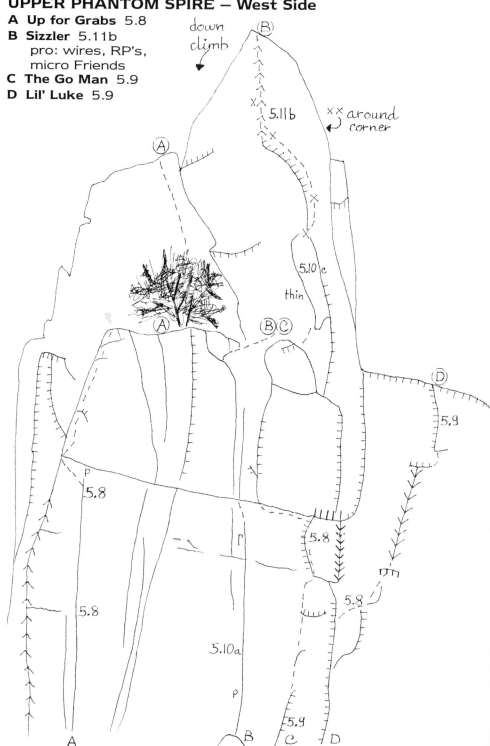

down climb

(B)

5.11b

x x around corner

(A)

5.10 c

thin

(A)

(B)(C)

(D)

5.9

p

5.8

5.8

5.8

5.8

5.8

5.10a

p

5.9

A   B   C   D

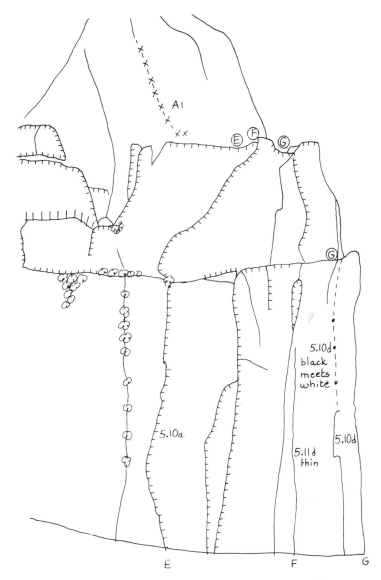

UPPER PHANTOM SPIRE — West Side

E Crispy Critters 5.10a

F Well Done 5.11d pro: Friends, wires

G Char Broiled 5.10d pro: Friends, wires, ⅜" slings

FLAT HEAD

On the east side of the rock is a prominent chimney. An awkward chockstone halfway up is 5.6. On the west side is a short roof and thin crack problem, 5.9.

LOST JOHN

On the steep south face of this rock is:

Turning Point 5.10b

MIDDLE PHANTOM SPIRE — North and West Sides

A Over Easy 5.7 pro: to 2½"
B Hard-Up variation 5.9 pro: to 2½"
C Slow Dancer 5.9
D Lean and Mean 5.9 pro: to 2½"   variation 5.11 top rope
E Cornflakes 5.9 variations 5.9
F Fancy Dancin' 5.10
G Candy Land 5.10c pro: thin nuts, runners

Ham and Eggs 5.9 A1
Immediately south of Middle Spire is a small buttress with a prominent large roof on its west side. Use a ramp (5.7) to gain the ledge beneath the roof, then use a few moves of aid to get over it. Finish with a finger crack.

Harding's Other Chimney 5.6
This route follows the obvious cleft on the west side of the buttress described previously.

photo: Harvey Overland

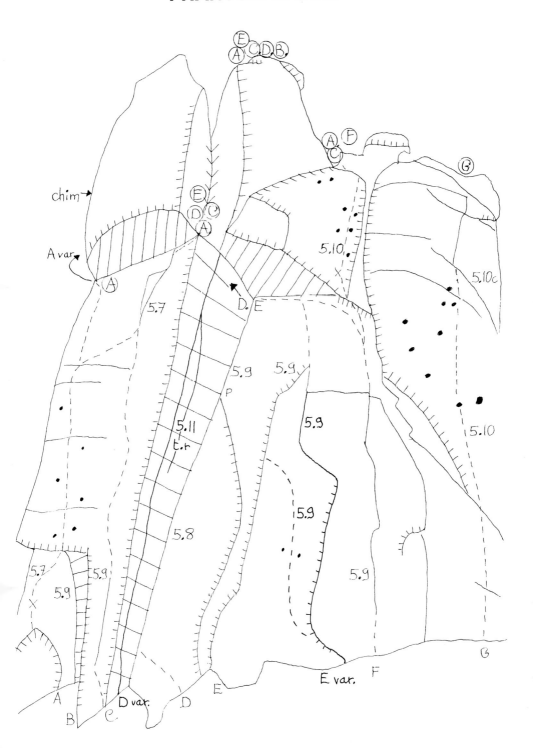

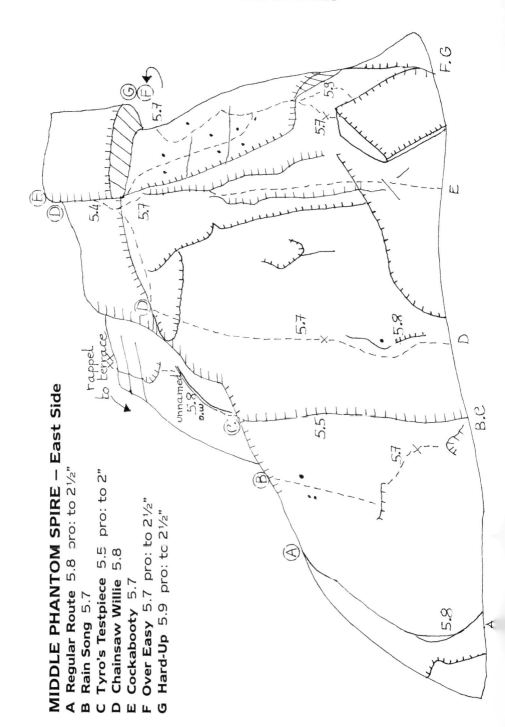

MIDDLE PHANTOM SPIRE – East Side

A **Regular Route** 5.8 pro: to 2½"
B **Rain Song** 5.7
C **Tyro's Testpiece** 5.5 pro: to 2"
D **Chainsaw Willie** 5.8
E **Cockabooty** 5.7
F **Over Easy** 5.7 pro: to 2½"
G **Hard-Up** 5.9 pro: to 2½"

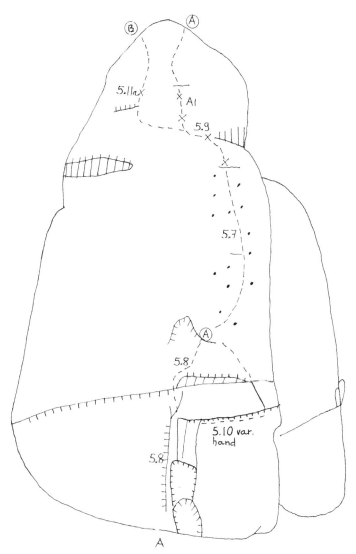

LOWER PHANTOM SPIRE — South Side

A Day Dreams 5.9 A1 variation 5.10 pro: to 1½", long dong
B Wet Dreams (variation) 5.11a

Regular Route 5.9 pro: to 3"
The route starts in the notch on the northwest side of the spire.
Climb a short thin crack (5.9) to a narrow ledge and traverse right
around a corner to a thin flake. Move right into a shallow, flared
chimney, follow it to easier ground just below the summit.
Abun-Daba variation 5.8 pro: to 3"
From the right hand margin of the northwest face, climb directly
to the summit from the traverse ledge. This climb is steep and
the lead committing.

LOWER PHANTOM SPIRE — East Side

A K.E. Cracks 5.11 pro: many wires
B Stage Fright 5.9 pro: to 3", rurps to med. angles
C Jack Corner 5.9 pro: to 2½"

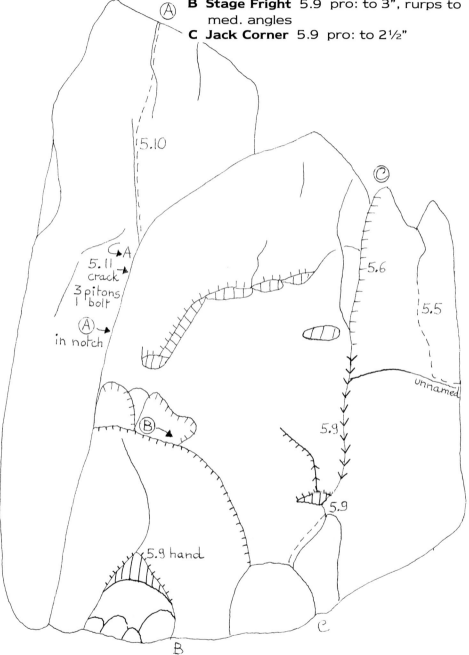

5.10

C A
5.11 crack
3 pitons 1 bolt

A → in notch

5.6

5.5

unnamed

B →

5.9

5.9

5.9 hand

B

C

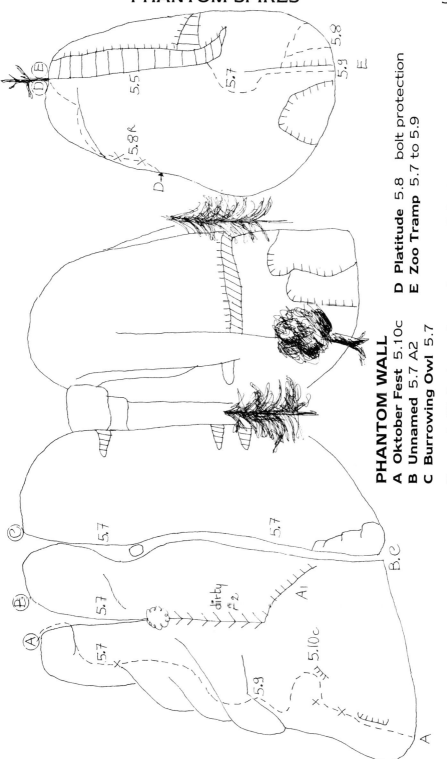

PHANTOM WALL

A Oktober Fest 5.10c   **D** Platitude 5.8   bolt protection

B Unnamed 5.7 A2   **E** Zoo Tramp 5.7 to 5.9

C Burrowing Owl 5.7

Descent: Walk down from the top of the boulder.

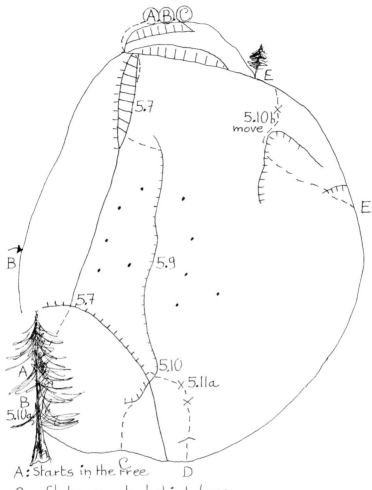

A: Starts in the tree
B: flake-crack behind tree

PHANTOM WALL — Right Hand Buttress
A Oedipus Rex 5.7
B La Chute 5.10a
C Electra 5.9 A2   variation 5.11a
D Dr. Jeckel and Mr. Hide 5.11a   This is a free variation of **Electra**.
E Eraser Head 5.10b

Descent: walk off the back side.

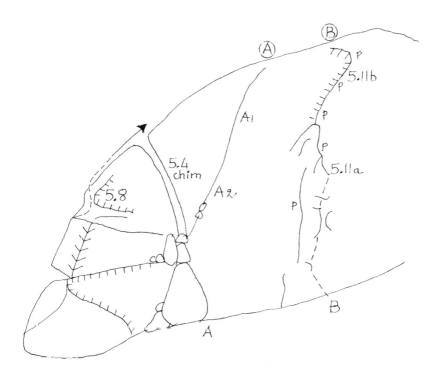

HOLIDAY ROCK — North Side

A Blue Tango A2
B Singe City 5.11b pro: RP's, wires, Friends to #1½

July 5.8
Start in a chimney on the right side of the east face. Ascend a pitch to a good ledge on the north side. The final pitch goes up and left to the top.

101 Dalmatians 5.10c   pro: many ⁹⁄₁₆" runners
Start just left of **July** and climb the steep knobby wall above, using bolts and slung knobs for protection.

Descent: walk off the back side.

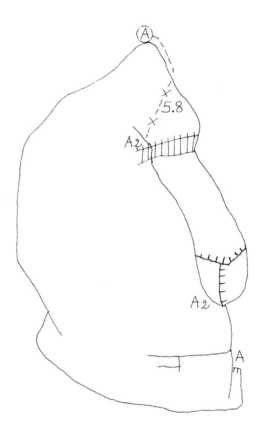

GORILLA ROCK — South Side
A Joe Young 5.8 A2

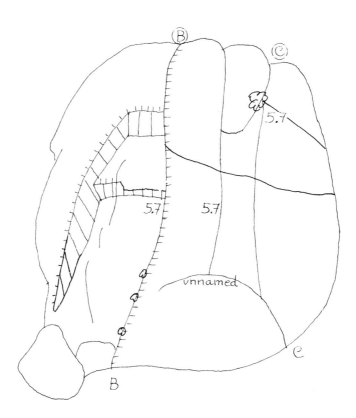

GORILLA ROCK — East Side
B Ko-Ko Box 5.7
C Ant Crack 5.7

Descent: rappel off a horn.

LOVER'S LEAP

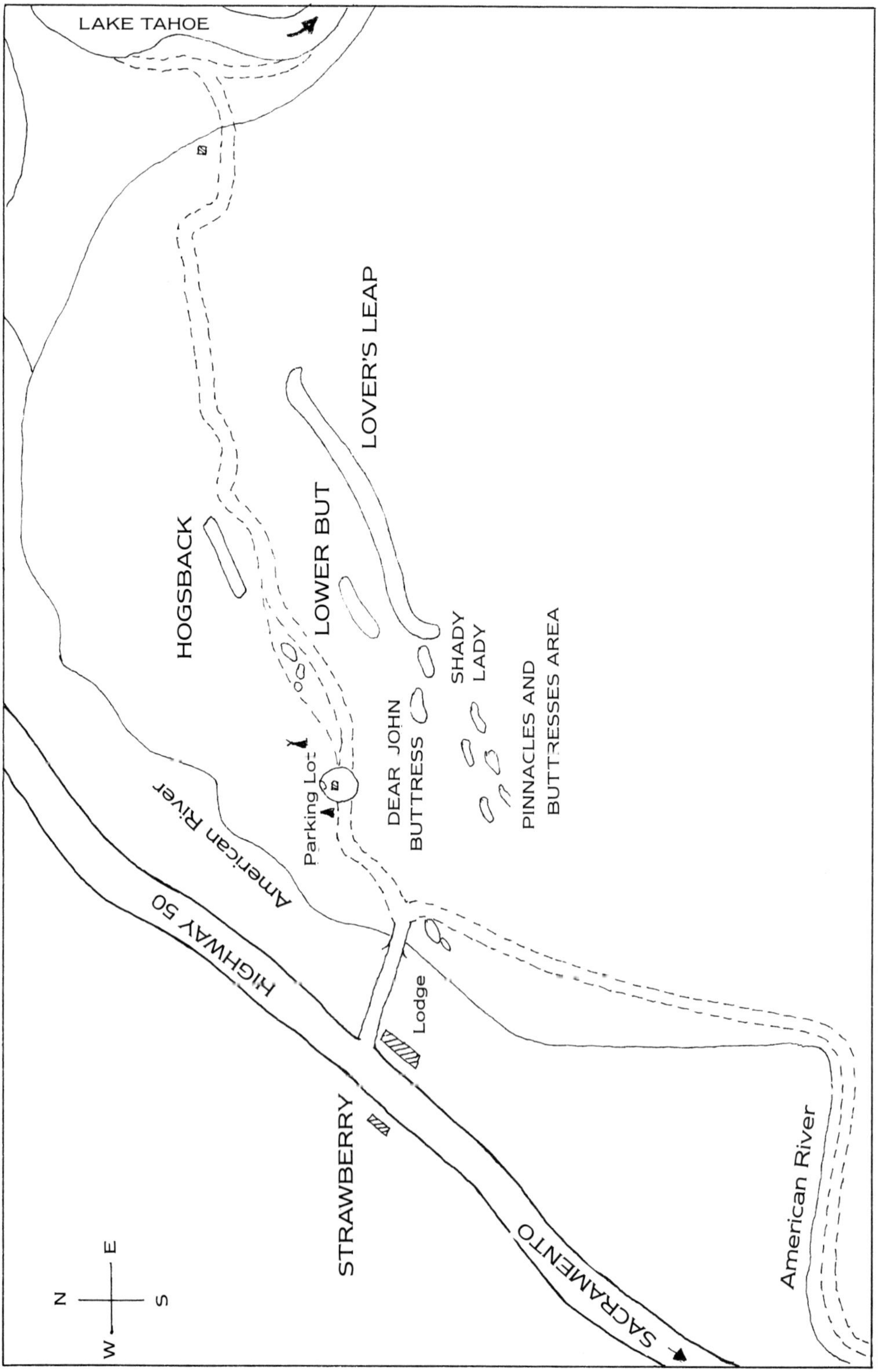
LAKE TAHOE
LOVER'S LEAP
LOWER BUT
HOGSBACK
SHADY LADY
DEAR JOHN BUTTRESS
PINNACLES AND BUTTRESSES AREA
Parking Lot
American River
HIGHWAY 50
Lodge
STRAWBERRY
SACRAMENTO
American River
N
E
S
W

LOVER'S LEAP

This unique and beautiful cliff is by far the most famous crag in the Tahoe region. Its steep wall rises behind and eastward of Strawberry Lodge on Highway 50, 18 miles southwest of Lake Tahoe and 40 miles east of Placerville. The 1/4 mile long, north facing wall reaches 600 feet in height at its western end and 350 feet at its eastern end. Lover's Leap is made of a special type of granite, striped with horizontal dikes. These dikes are rich in quartz and feldspar and have eroded more slowly than the rest of the rock, forming protrusions ranging in width from small bulges to ledges more than ten inches wide. The dikes are abundant and make the climbing at Lover's Leap unique. Much vertical terrain that would otherwise be virtually impossible to free climb is rendered easy by these dikes.

Lover's Leap is very popular. The climbs are numerous, of good quality, well protected, and cover a full range of difficulty, from easy to very hard. Access to the cliff is simple and short, there is a free campground, and the beautiful and historic Strawberry Lodge is only a mile from the rock.

To reach the parking area or the campground, drive toward the cliff on a small road that starts in front of the Lodge. Cross a small bridge over the American River and turn left onto a pebbly road. Follow this road into the forest where it turns into a one-way loop. Camping and parking spots are located on both sides of this loop. To get to the base of the climbs, take a sandy path which starts from the eastern apex of the road loop, across from the toilets, and follow it for 1/4 mile to some big boulders. Pass these boulders and keep walking east on a rocky road (which is a streambed in the spring). Incidentally, this rocky little road is part of the original Pony Express Trail that followed the American River down to Sacramento. The approach to the Lower Buttress starts 50 yards up the road to the right, via a small trail that leads through the manzanitas. To reach the main cliff, continue up the rocky road, where one will periodically find trails branching off to the right, leading through openings in the manzanitas to the talus field where most climbers leave their packs and change into their climbing shoes. Small trails lead up through the talus to the bases of the climbs.

LOVER'S LEAP

photo: Bill Serniuk

The western section of the wall is bisected 150 feet off the ground by Main Ledge, which is the start of many of the routes on the upper wall. Main Ledge starts near the west end of the cliff and can be followed by 2nd or 3rd class for about 250 feet to the right hand corner of Eagle Buttress. A loose 5.8/5.9 traverse can link you to the rest of Main Ledge, which continues to just past **Bookmark.** Main Ledge can be reached either by hiking up a long talus fan and trail on the west or by climbing any of several routes which begin at the base of the West Wall.

To descend from any of the routes ending on top of the crag, follow a trail leading east through the bushes and forest behind the top of the cliff. Make sure that you follow this trail and **not** the one leading south from the top of the West Wall. At the far eastern end the trail crosses a small creek. (The water in this creek is so far safe for drinking; please take care that it stays this way.) Turn left and descend, step back across the creek and continue to descend along the eastern edge of the lower slabs. At the bottom of the slabs a trail leads through the trees back to the Pony Express Trail.

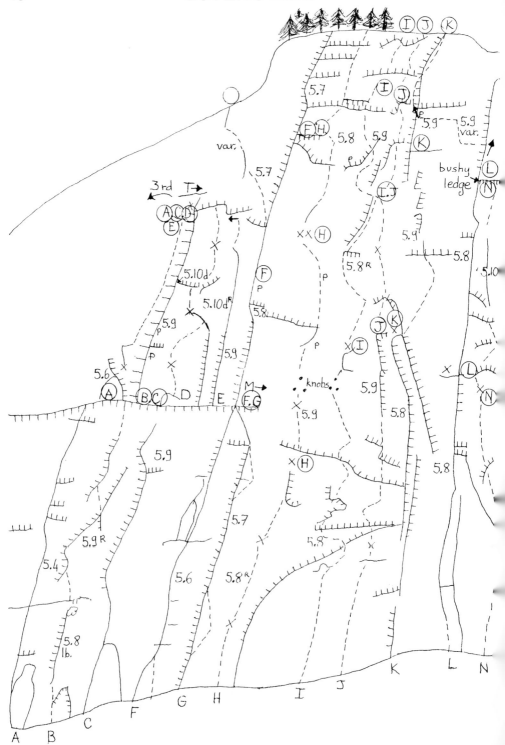

EAST WALL — East Part

A Pop Bottle 5.6 pro: to 2½"
B Far East 5.9 pro: to 1"
C East Corner 5.10d pro: to 2"
D Out to Lunge 5.10d R pro: tiny to ⅓"
E Rednecks 5.9 pro: to 1½"
F Haystack 5.8 pro: to 2"
G Preparation H 5.8 pro: to 2½"
H Fear No Evil 5.9 R pro: to 2"
I Fantasia 5.9 R pro: to 2½", ½" webbing loops
J The Last Sandwich 5.9 pro: small Friends
K Scimitar 5.9 pro: to 2"
L East Crack 5.8 pro: to 2½"
M M.D.A. start 5.9 R pro: to 2"
This route is a traverse of all the first belay stances of all the routes on the East Wall from left to right.
N Between the Lines 5.10a
T High Tour start 5.9 pro: to 2"
This is a traverse of all the second belay stances of all the routes on the East Wall from left to right.

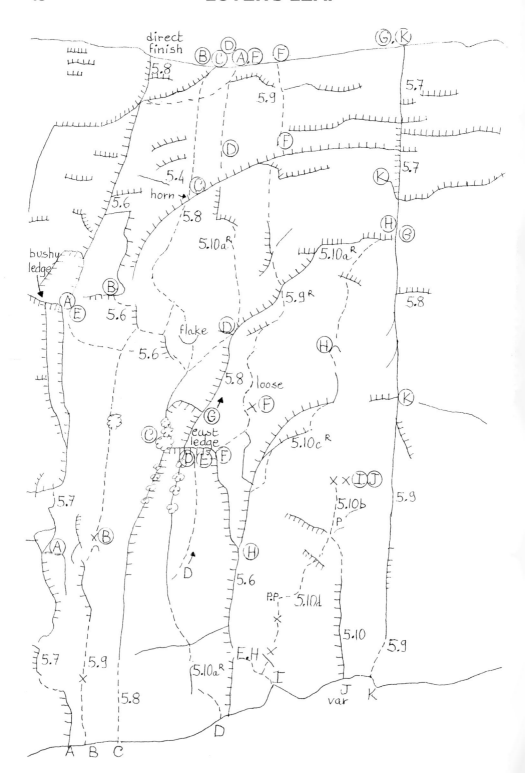

photo: Christine Jenkewitz-Meytras

EAST WALL – Middle Part

A Bear's Reach 5.7
B Ham Sandwich 5.9
C Horn Blower 5.8 pro: to 2½"
D Pigs on the Wing 5.10a R pro: to 1½", slings
E East Wall 5.6 pro: to 2½"
F Fireworks 5.9 R pro: to 2½"
G Flying Circus 5.10a R pro: to 3"
H Bad Moon Arising 5.10c pro: Friends to #2
I Easier Said Than Done 5.10d pro: to #2 Friend
J End of the Line 5.10b
K The Line 5.9 pro: to 2½"

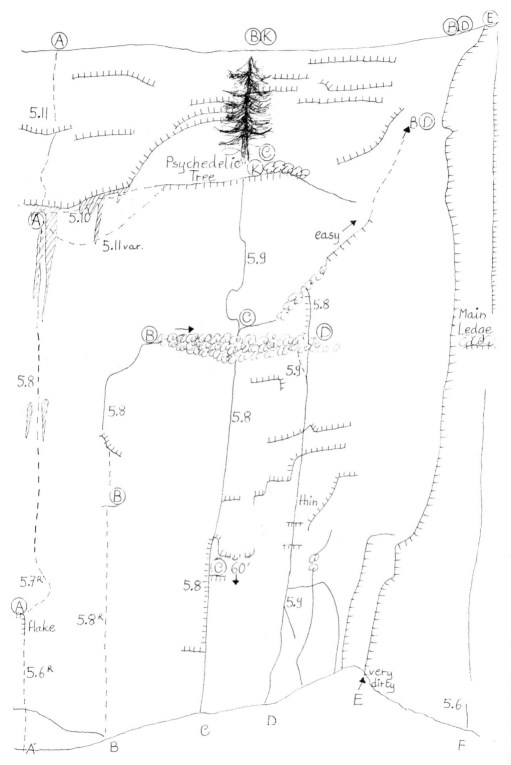

EAST WALL — West Part

A A Few Dollars More 5.10/5.11 pro: to 2"
B Deviate 5.8 pro: to 2"
C Psychedelic 5.9 pro: to 2½"
D Fandango 5.9 pro: to 2"
E East Gully 5.6 pro: to 3"
F Paramour 5.9   pro: to 3"

This route is very vegetated. Climb the first crack right of **East Gully**. Follow the crack and climb on the face to avoid bushy sections (5.9) to a ledge atop a left facing corner. Climb up a gully to Main Ledge. Ascend a difficult three inch crack and follow a left facing dihedral to the rim.

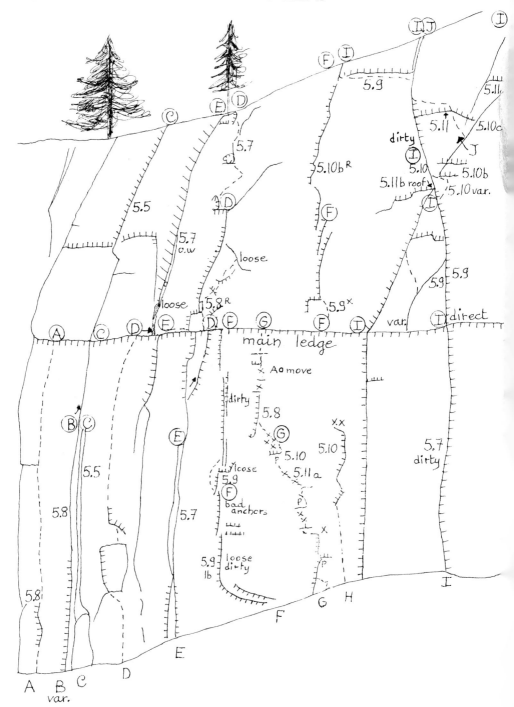

5.9

5.11c

5.7

5.5

dirty

5.11

5.10c

5.10b R

5.10

J

5.10b

5.11b roof

5.10 var.

5.7
o.w

loose

5.9

5.9

loose

5.8 R

main ledge

var.

direct

Ao move

dirty

5.8

x.x

5.5

5.10

5.10

5.8

loose

5.9

5.11a

5.7
dirty

bad
anchors

5.7

5.9
lb

loose
dirty

F

G H

I

A   B   C

var.

D

E

The Slash

Rat's Tooth

The Wedge

The Big Top →

← April Fools

West Wall

Main Ledge

Main Line

Tombstone Ledge →

Traveller Buttress

photo: Bill Serniuk

CENTRAL WALL

A Skyrocket 5.8 pro: to 2"
B Bastard Child 5.8 pro: to 2½"
C Lover's Chimney 5.5 pro: to 3"
D Sudden Death 5.8 R pro: to 2"
E Bookmark 5.7 pro: to 3"
F Incubus 5.10b X pro: to 2"
G Glaze-Her-Face 5.11a A1 pro: to 2"
H Unknown 5.10
I Rated X Direct 5.11b R
J Tic-Tic-Tic 5.11a

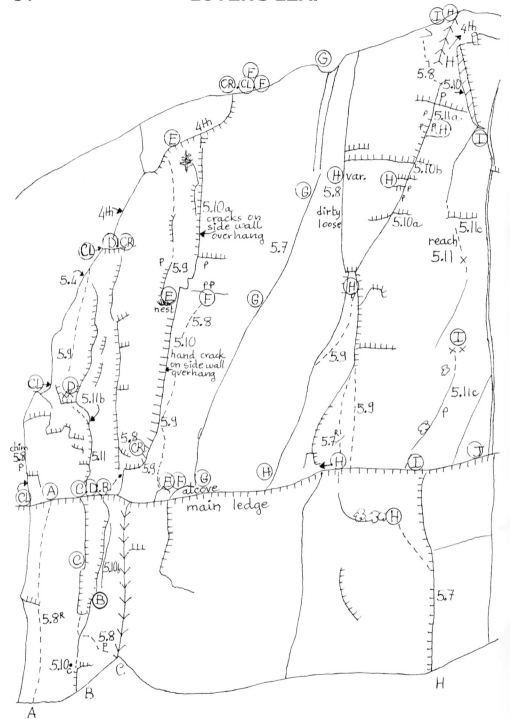

CENTRAL WALL

A Eagle's Highway 5.8 R pro: webbing slings
B Roofer Madness 5.10c pro: to 2"
CL Eagle Buttress, left hand side 5.8 pro: to 3"
CR Eagle Buttress, right hand side 5.9 pro: to 3"
D More Madness 5.11b
E Flying High 5.10a
F Excelsior 5.10a pro: to 3"
G East of Eyore 5.8
H The Hourglass 5.11a (5.8 var.) pro: to 3"
I Hourglass Wall 5.11c
J Eyore's Ecstacy 5.7 pro: to 3"

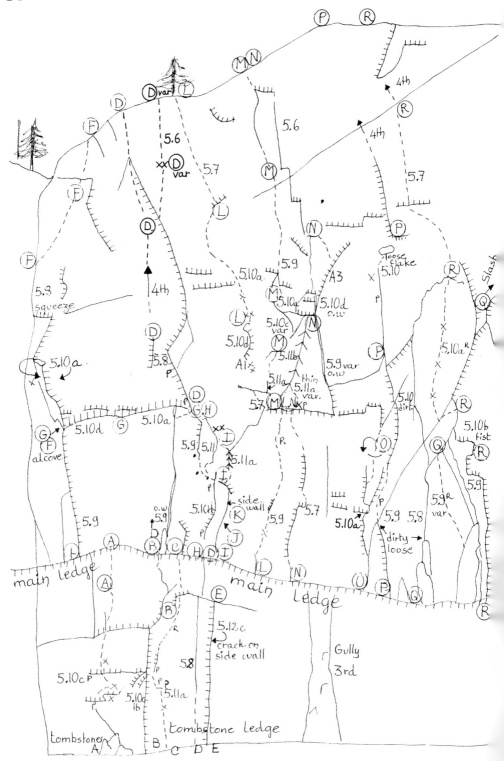

MAIN WALL

Below Main Ledge

A Epitaph 5.10c

B Tombstone Terror 5.10c pro: to 2½"

C Boothill 5.11a

D Traveller Buttress 5.9

E The Silly Willy Crack 5.12c

Above Main Ledge

F Eyore's Enigma 5.10a pro: to 4"

G Under The Big Top 5.10d pro: wires, 3 sets
  Friends to #4

H Purple Haze 5.10d pro: to 2½"

I Variation, Cross Town Traffic 5.11a

J Corrugation Corner 5.7 pro: to 2½" vars. 5.8, 5.9

K Crash Landing 5.10a R pro: #2 RP's to #3 Friends

L Up From the Skies 5.10d

M Wall Flower 5.10a (5.10c var.) pro: to 3", mainly small

N North Face 5.11 (5.9 A3 var.) pro: to 2½"

O Cheap Shot 5.10a

P North Country 5.10 dirty and loose pro: to 3"

Q The Slash 5.9 (5.9 var.)

R Bombs Away 5.10b pro: small wires, Friends to #4

The Rat's Tooth fell off in the summer of 1986.

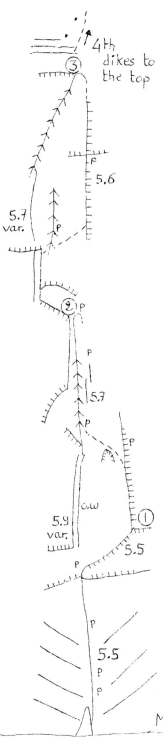

4th dikes to the top

③

5,6

5.7 var.

② P

P

5.7

P

P

c.w

5.9 var.

① 5.5

P

5.5

P

P

Main Ledge

MAIN WALL
J Corrugation Corner 5.7
   (5.8, 5.9 vars.)
   pro: to 2½"

LOVER'S LEAP — Main Wall   photo: Bill Serniuk

LOVER'S LEAP

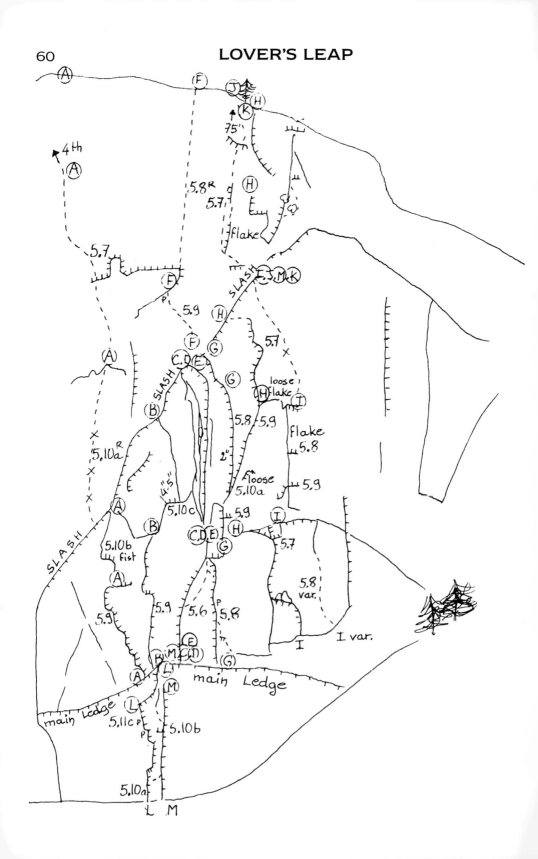

WEST WALL

Above Main Ledge

A Bombs Away 5.10b   pro: small wires, Friends to #4

B Arrowroot 5.10c   pro: to 3½"

C West Wall 5.8 pro: to 4"

D Crazy Daze 5.9   pro: to 3"

E Hospital Corner 5.10a   pro: to 1½"

F Al Tahoe 5.9

G The Gamoke 5.8   pro: to 2"

H Last Laugh 5.10a   pro: to 2"

I April Fools 5.8 pro: to 3"

J Dead Tree Direct 5.7   pro: to 3"

K Easier Than it Looks 5.7

Start right of **Dead Tree Direct**. Dikes and horns lead up into a chimney. Exit right from the top of the chimney, then up and left to the top of **Dead Tree Direct**.

Below Main Ledge

L Main Line 5.11c   pro: to 2½"

M Magnum Force 5.10b   pro: to 1½"

WEST WALL
A Craven Image 5.7 pro: to 3"
B The Clonedike 5.9
C Captain Coconuts 5.10a   Follow the arete of **Vanishing Point.**
   pro: thin wires, RP's
D Vanishing Point 5.10b pro: to 4"
E Ozzie 5.10a pro: thin wires, RP's
F Third Stone from the Sun 5.10c pro: to 4"
G The Banana 5.8 pro: to 2½"

Shorts Only 5.8
This is the right side of **The Banana.** The first pitch starts at a bush and involves jamming a loose pillar and a 5.7 flake. A short 5.8 offwidth section in a dihedral is found on the second pitch. On the third pitch, ascend easy rock then traverse up and left through brush. The final pitch involves difficult stemming over an overhang.

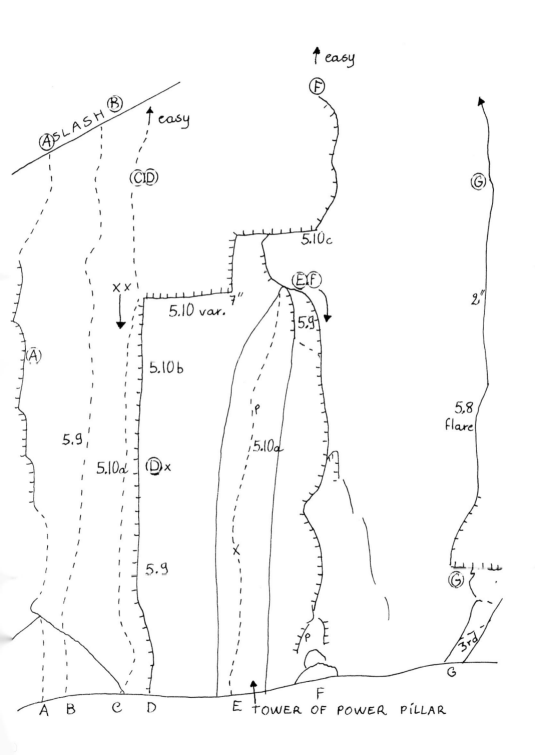

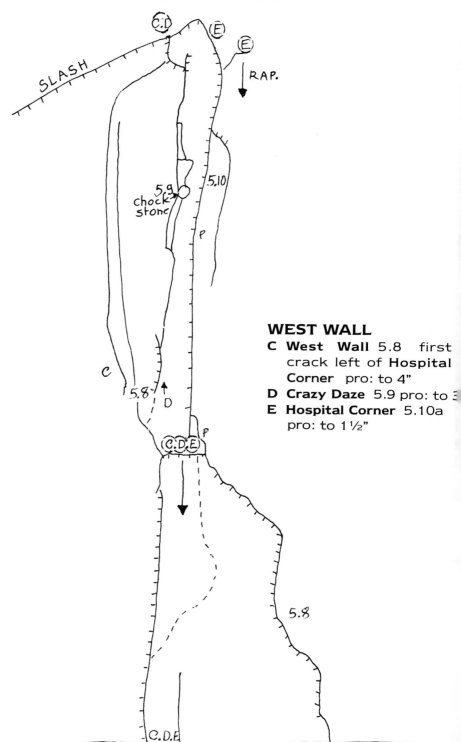

SLASH

RAP.

5.10

5.9
chock
stone

c

5.8

D

P

C.D.E

5.8

C.D.E

WEST WALL
C West Wall 5.8   first
crack left of **Hospital
Corner** pro: to 4"
D Crazy Daze 5.9 pro: to
E Hospital Corner 5.10a
pro: to 1½"

LOWER BUTTRESS   photo: Bill Serniuk

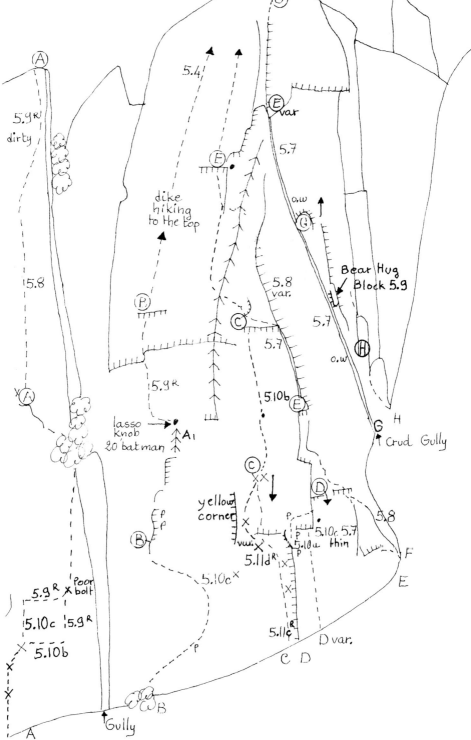

(A)

5.9ʀ dirty

15.8

(A)

(A)

5.9ᴿ Poor bolt

5.10c 5.9ᴿ

5.10b

A

Gully

B

(P)

5.9ᴿ

lasso knob
20 batman

A₁

(B)

(C)

yellow corner

var.

5.11dᴿ

5.10c

P

5.4

dike hiking to the top

(E)

(E) var

5.7

(G)

o.w

Bear Hug Block 5.9

5.7

5.8 var.

5.7

5.10b

(E)

(C)

(D)

5.10c 5.7 thin

5.10a

5.11c

D var.

C D

o.w

(H)

H

G Crud Gully

5.8

F

E

G

LOWER BUTTRESS

The Lower Buttress sits below the West Wall of Lover's Leap. It is a tri-pillared formation whose 300 foot north faces are striped with dikes. The routes are excellent. Approach to the Pony Express Trail as for the main cliffs, but walk right 50 yards to a small trail that heads up to the base of the wall. Descend from the top by walking west on ramps and blocks and through bushes (class 3). After 50 yards it becomes easy to cut back and contour down along the base of the rock.

A Beer Can Alley 5.10c   pro: small to 1"
B Piece of Mind 5.10c A1 X
C Pillar of Society 5.11 R
D Surrealistic Pillar Direct 5.10a (5.10c var.) pro: to 3"
E Surrealistic Pillar Regular Route 5.7 pro: to 3"
F Jailbreak (5.8 var.)   pro: to 1½"
G For Real Crack 5.7 pro: to 3"
H Bearhug 5.9 pro: to 2½"
Scramble up **Crud Gully,** past **For Real Crack,** to the base of a right facing corner capped by a ceiling. A giant horn must be bearhugged (5.9) twenty feet higher. Step right into a long crack just before reaching the ceiling. Belay after the overhang. Climb up the slab above, passing a large overhang on its left side (5.8).

Flaky Flakes 5.10b
Start 100 feet up and left of **Beer Can Alley** on a lieback flake. Ascend the middle of the face. Loose holds allow nuts protection.

Crawdaddys in Flight 5.10c
This route climbs a 10 foot ceiling on the right side of a small outcrop above Lower Buttress.

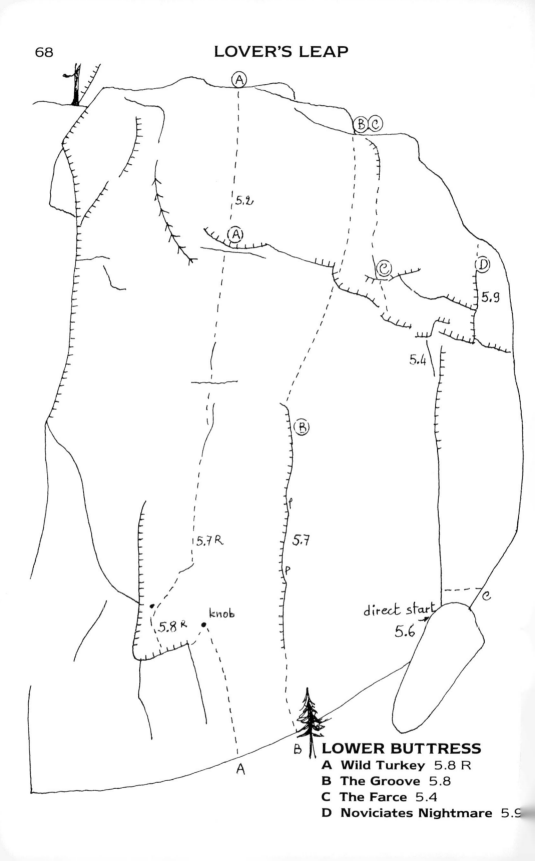

LOWER BUTTRESS
A **Wild Turkey** 5.8 R
B **The Groove** 5.8
C **The Farce** 5.4
D **Noviciates Nightmare** 5.9

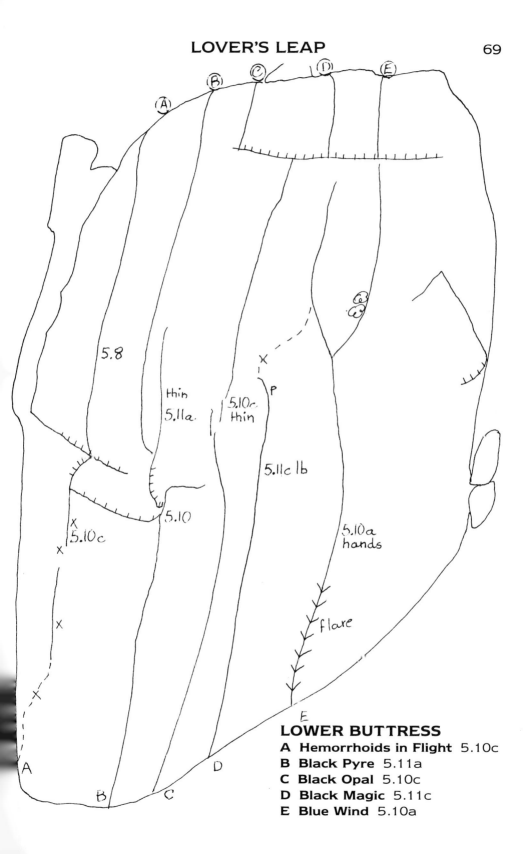

5.8

thin
5.11a.

5.10c
thin

P

5.11c 1b

5.10
X
5.10c
X

X
5.10a
hands

flare

E

LOWER BUTTRESS
A Hemorrhoids in Flight 5.10c
B Black Pyre 5.11a
C Black Opal 5.10c
D Black Magic 5.11c
E Blue Wind 5.10a

A

B   C   D

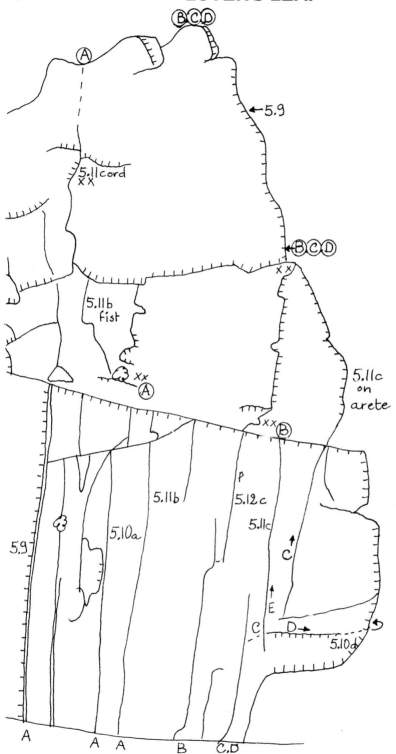

Ⓐ Ⓑ Ⓒ Ⓓ

← 5.9

5.11 cord
xx

Ⓑ Ⓒ Ⓓ
xx

5.11b
fist

5.11c
on
arete

Ⓐ
xx

xx Ⓑ

5.9

5.10a

5.11b

p
5.12c

5.11c

C

E

C   D →

5.10d

A   A   A   B   C,D

DEAR JOHN BUTTRESS

Below and to the west of the western end of Lover's Leap stands Dear John Buttress. It is a 200 foot high crag, the east face of which is gently overhanging. The granite is good and offers some very good crack climbs. To reach the rock, take the small trail that leads to the Lower Buttress, then hike up and around to the right until you are level with Dear John Buttress. An indistinct trail leads right to the base of the crag.

A God of Thunder 5.11b   pro: to 5"
B Stone Cold Crazy 5.12c
C Drug Crazed 5.11c
D Stony End 5.11c
E Stony Highway 5.11c

Stony God 5.11d/5.12a
This is a combination of the first pitch of **God of Thunder** and the second half of **Stone Cold Crazy**.

Walk off the summit.

SHADY LADY

Shady Lady is a buttress-like formation located uphill from Dear John Buttress. It is best approached from the top of the Lower Buttress in the vicinity of **The Farce**. Walk up in the direction of Dear John Buttress, passing that to reach the base of the face. The descent is made by walking down the gully on the left.

Shady Lady 5.8
This is a long pitch up the obvious curvy crack that splits the face.
Dirty Harry 5.9   pro: to 2"
A nice pitch ascends a crack in a corner on the left side of the Shady Lady Buttress.
The Sickle 5.8   pro: to 3"
Follow the sickle-shaped crack on the buttress.

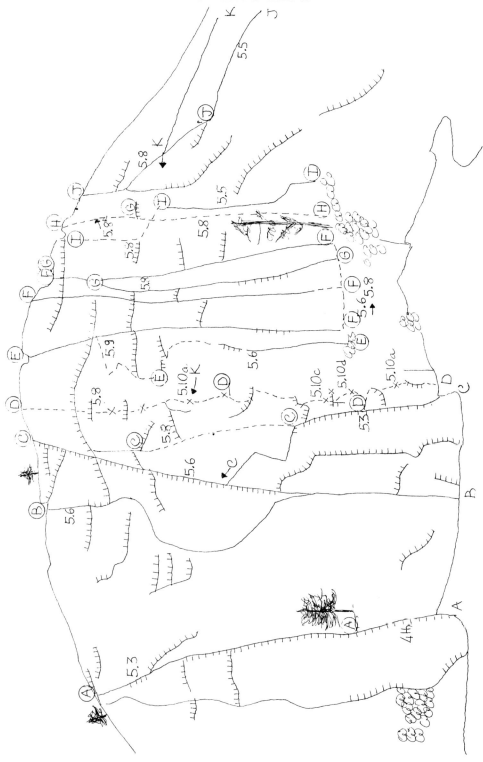

HOGSBACK

The Hogsback is a long, slabby, low angle ridge capped with small overhangs that sits on the north side of the Pony Express Trail, opposite Lover's Leap. It is good ground for beginners but hard face and friction climbs have been done. Most of the routes are on the north side, overlooking Highway 50. The south side slabs provide sunny vantage points for studying the routes on Lover's Leap.

A **Knapsack Crack** 5.3 pro: to 2"
B **Red's Delight** 5.9 pro: to 1"
C **Deception** 5.6 (Direct 5.8) pro: to 2½"
D **Dancin' Feet** 5.10d pro: thin
E **Settle Down** 5.9 pro: to 2"

Red's Delight 5.9 pro: 1"
This is an obscure line. Climb up and left of **Deception's** two parallel cracks for 80 feet, then move up and left to a belay stance on top of blocks. Climb up and left for forty feet to a bolt. Continue straight up (5.9) to another bolt, 30 feet above the first one. Climb up to a right facing and leaning corner. Continue straight up to a belay stance in a left facing corner. The last pitch goes straight up to the top (5.6).

F **Harvey's Wallbangers** 5.6-5.8
G **Pips Pillar** 5.8
H **Carly Ann's Butterflies** 5.8 R pro: to 2½"
I **Manic Depressive** 5.8
J **Wave Rider** 5.8 oro: to 1½"
K **Crazy Lace** 5.9 pro: to 2"

This is a fine girdle traverse. Start near mid-height on the north face and follow a dike and thin crack that runs toward the middle of the face to a bolt. Climb up and over an overhang and diagonal left to the second belay of **Wave Rider**. Move down and left and climb under an overhang to reach a dihedral. Contine left on a 5.9 face to reach a belay bolt. Climb straight left for 50 feet (5.9) to reach a bolt and then climb 50 feet higher to a good belay stance. The last pitch is easy 5th class and coincides with the top part of **Deception**.

THE HOGSBACK　　　photo: Bill Serniuk

HOGSBACK

The following climbs are found at the western end, around on the southwest side of Hogsback, and are not included in the topos.

Jeff's Folly 5.7

This route lies several hundred feet west of **Crazy Lace,** where the face becomes compact and steeper. The four pitches are consistently moderate.

The Number 5.7

This three pitch route follows an indistinct line to the right of **Jeff's Folly.**

Peanut Brittle 5.7   195' pro: to 2½"

This route starts below a windblown tree on the only steep rock on Hogback's south face. Climb up left on a sloping ramp/ledge to reach a crack that goes up the left side of a smooth slab. From the top of the slab climb up to a belay at the windblown tree. A short 4th class pitch finishes the route. **Variation 5.8** From the top of the smooth slab, undercling an overhang to the right. Follow a right facing and leaning arch system.

Raspberry Bypass 5.10b   200' pro: to 1½"

A steep face 15 feet left of the start of **Peanut Brittle** leads to a left slanting ramp. A bolt 15 feet off the ground protects the crux moves. The ramp is 5.9 and leads to easier rock. Stay left of **Peanut Brittle** all the way to the top.

Strawberry Overpass 5.10b   one pitch

To the left of **Raspberry Bypass** is this beautiful face climb. A bolt 20 feet off the ground is followed by easier climbing to the top.

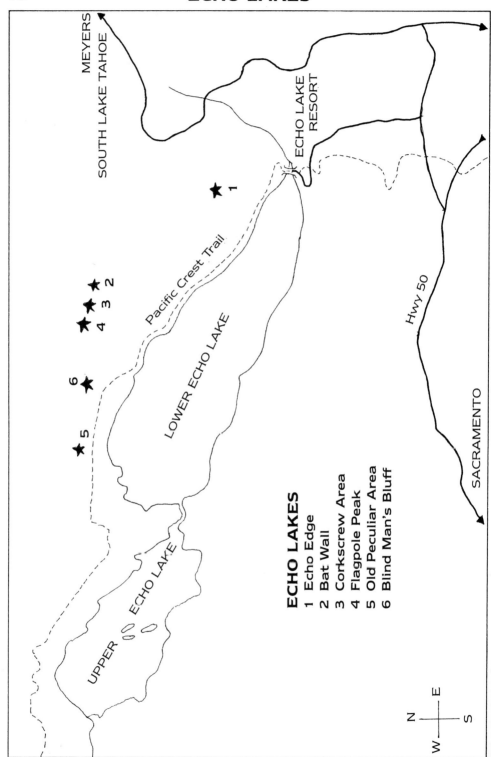

ECHO LAKES
1 Echo Edge
2 Bat Wall
3 Corkscrew Area
4 Flagpole Peak
5 Old Peculiar Area
6 Blind Man's Bluff

ECHO LAKES

To reach Echo Lakes follow Highway 50 for two miles west of Echo Summit. Turn north on a road marked "Berkeley — Echo Lake Campground"; follow this road for two miles to the edge of lower Echo Lake, where you will find a lodge and a small marina. Park in either of the two available paved parking areas.

All of the climbing crags are found along the north shore of lower Echo Lake. A well-marked and well-travelled trail leads west from the lodge along the north side of the lake, making all the approaches fairly easy. The closest cliff, Echo Edge, at an elevation of 7700 feet, is within a quarter mile of the lodge, its base only about 100 feet above the trail. Flagpole Peak, at 8363 feet, is the highest point along this rocky ridge and is one mile from the lodge. Its name comes from a metal flagpole that has been placed at the summit and is just visible from the trail. Bat Wall and the Corkscrew Area, lesser cliffs, form the south face of Flagpole Peak's long east ridge. Blind Man's Bluff and the Old Peculiar Area are the westernmost crags, standing above the far end of the lake. The rock here ranges from solid granite to rough and coarse-grained stone which is crumbly in places. Generally, the rock improves with altitude. With the notable exceptions of **E.B.'s Wall** and the extraordinary **Kangaroo**, the climbs follow crack systems.

ECHO EDGE

photo: Bill Serniuk

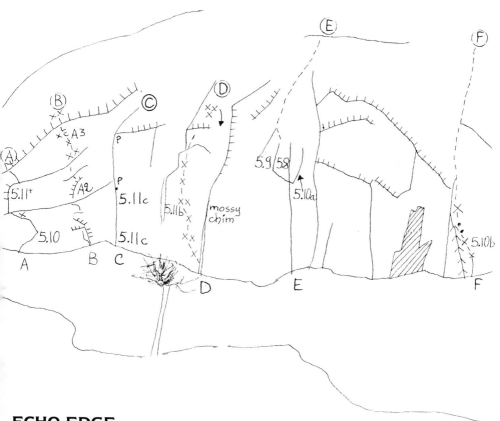

ECHO EDGE

This small cliff is only a few minutes' walk from the lodge along the trail. It is the first significant vertical relief one encounters when walking west. To descend from the top, walk northwest to the left corner of the rock and down a 3rd class slab.

A Little Sir Echo 5.11+ top rope
B Rehumanize Yourself A3 pro: copperheads, bathooks
C Bolt Race 5.11c
D We've Created a Monster 5.11b
E Pitchfork 5.8 to 5.10a
F E.B.'s Wall 5.10b pro: to 1½"

Dumbo 5.9
This is the chimney right of **Bolt Race**.

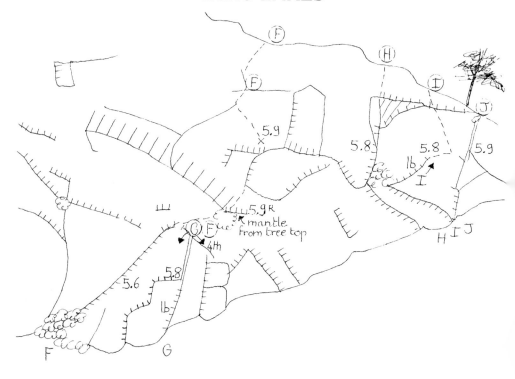

ECHO EDGE

F Rock-a-bye Baby 5.9 R
G Rough and Ready 5.8 pro: to 2½"
H Bushfreak Corner 5.8 pro: to 2"
I   Bushfreak Eliminate 5.8 pro: to 2"
J Squeeze and Wheeze 5.9 pro: to 2"

FLAGPOLE PEAK

photo: Bill Serniuk

This peak is at the crest of the ridge, one mile from the lodge. It has the highest face of all the cliffs in the Echo Lakes area. The rock improves as one climbs up and the granite of the last pitches is solid and compact. To reach the base, hike up the trail from the lodge for ¾ mile until you are below the face, then hike up the steep hillside toward the peak. The descent is made by walking down the 3rd class southeast ridge for several hundred feet, then scrambling down boulders and slabs toward the lake.

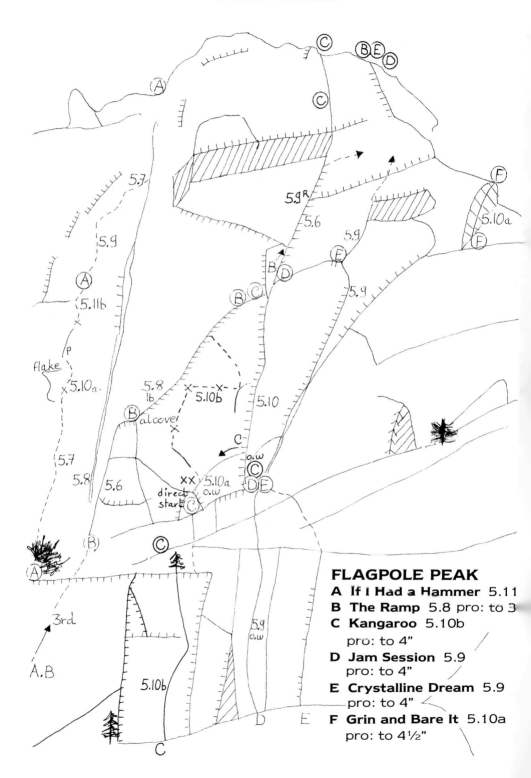

FLAGPOLE PEAK
A If I Had a Hammer 5.11
B The Ramp 5.8 pro: to 3
C Kangaroo 5.10b
      pro: to 4"
D Jam Session 5.9
      pro: to 4"
E Crystalline Dream 5.9
      pro: to 4"
F Grin and Bare It 5.10a
      pro: to 4½"

BLIND MAN'S BLUFF

photo: Bill Serniuk

BAT WALL

Bat Wall is located 100 yards down and to the right of the Corkscrew Area, on Flagpole Peak's southeast ridge. It is a narrow buttress traversed by a large ledge.

Aftermath 120' 5.9   chocks to 3½"
Above the right end of the large traversing ledge is a wide crack. Climb a flake into the crack. Near the top the crack passes through a bulge (5.9). Above, the top is reached by 3rd class terrain.

BLIND MAN'S BLUFF

This is a small cliff set back from the main trail that leads from the lodge. Walk past the west end of Flagpole Peak, then climb up switchbacks past large boulders. A cliff will appear above the trail; above this cliff is Blind Man's Bluff. The rock is excellent. To descend, walk down the north side toward the trail.

Magic Book 5.8   pro: to 3"
This is the first obvious corner on the left.
Bookie 5.10
Climb the corner to the right of **Magic Book.**
Pyramid 5.10
Start in **Bookie,** then climb the obvious crack up and around the arête to the summit, next to **Magic Book.**
Death Tuna 5.10   pro: wires, RP's and Friends
Start in **Bookie,** then go right to the thin crack on the prow. Finish on the knobby face or follow the crack.
Snake Charmer 5.11c   pro: thin wires, RP's
One hundred feet right of **Bookie,** climb the thin crack/dihedral to one bolt-protected face move at the top.
Golden Years 5.11a   pro: small Friends, RP's
Follow shallow corners up the hill from **Snake Charmer.**
Slithering Slit 5.5
This is the obvious easy chimney to the left of **Magic Book.**

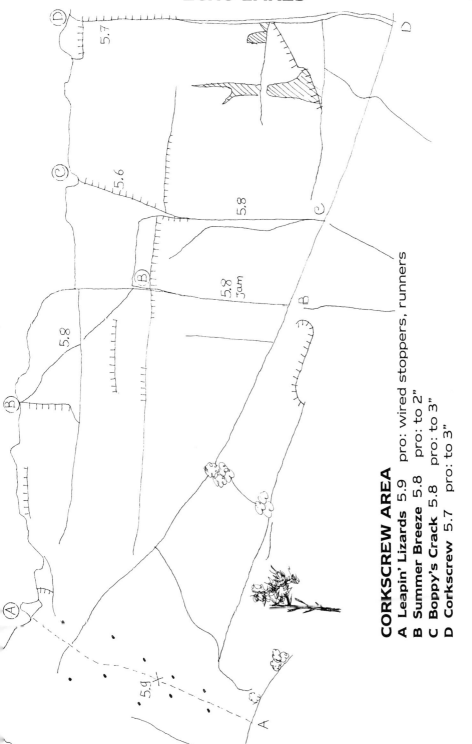

CORKSCREW AREA

A Leapin' Lizards 5.9   pro: wired stoppers, runners
B Summer Breeze 5.8   pro: to 2"
C Boppy's Crack 5.8   pro: to 3"
D Corkscrew 5.7   pro: to 3"

OLD PECULIAR AREA

From Blind Man's Bluff continue up the trail. In an open area short cliffs appear on the right, covered with cracks. Above and to the left is a north facing corner with a large cedar tree next to it. This is Old Peculiar Area. The granite is good.

Offwidth Their Heads 5.9   pro: to 4"
This is the prominent wide crack on the far left.

Sayonara 5.7   pro: to 2"
Climb left slanting cracks to a ramp. Follow the ramp to the base of a left slanting flake. Climb the flake to the top.

Yodeler 5.9   pro: to 2"
Start at the cedar tree. A 5.9 finger crack leads to a slot. Follow it to the top.

Old Peculiar 5.8   pro: to 3½"
This is the corner where the two walls meet. A few awkward moves are encountered before reaching the top.

Knee-On 5.10b   pro: to 5"
This route starts ten feet right of the corner. It is a hard jam crack and the crux is the moves leading to a ledge halfway up.

Mangod 5.11a
Above Meyers Grade to Echo Summit, on Highway 50, is a prominent gray slab with a left facing corner on its right side. Take a line up the center of the slab. The crux involves steep face climbing on micro flakes. Approach by going either straight up the hill from the platform used to shoot avalanches, or by proceeding to the gap between Echo Edge and Flagpole Peak and dropping down benches to the largest slab. To descend, walk off the climb.

THE PIE SHOP photo: Bill Serniuk

THE PIE SHOP

The Pie Shop is the western peak of a rock formation listed on the map as "Twin Peaks." Its light granite face has a southerly exposure and therefore permits warm and sunny climbing all year round. Just a mile from the city of South Lake Tahoe, this is a popular and easily accessible area. Take Highway 50 west from the junction of Highway 50 and Highway 89 North, at the "Y" in Lake Tahoe. Shortly past the airport, turn right on Sawmill Road before crossing the bridge over the South Fork of the Upper Truckee River. Park ¼ mile up Sawmill Road, across from two houses on the right. Hike up the hillside to the right of the houses, passing big boulders, and angle up right to find a small trail that leads to the left corner of the peak.

A huge boulder with a perfectly flat top (Lunch Rock) lies at the left corner base of the rock. Most climbers leave their packs here and follow little trails along the base to their chosen climbs.

The rock is good to excellent, with cracks and knobby faces, but it can be coarse and hard on the hands. Protection is easily obtained in the numerous cracks, and bolts are found on some routes. The climbs reach up to 230 feet in height and cover the full range of difficulty, including some aid problems.

To descend, walk northwest along the top to the ravine that separates the two peaks, descend and cut right as soon as possible to get back to the trail along the base. Follow this trail past the Marmot Cave and it will lead back to Lunch Rock.

The Pie Shop is also famous for its giant boulderfield, which extends completely around the west peak. Excellent and varied problems can be found at Echo View Estates and off Sawmill Road. See the **BOULDERING AREAS** section for more details.

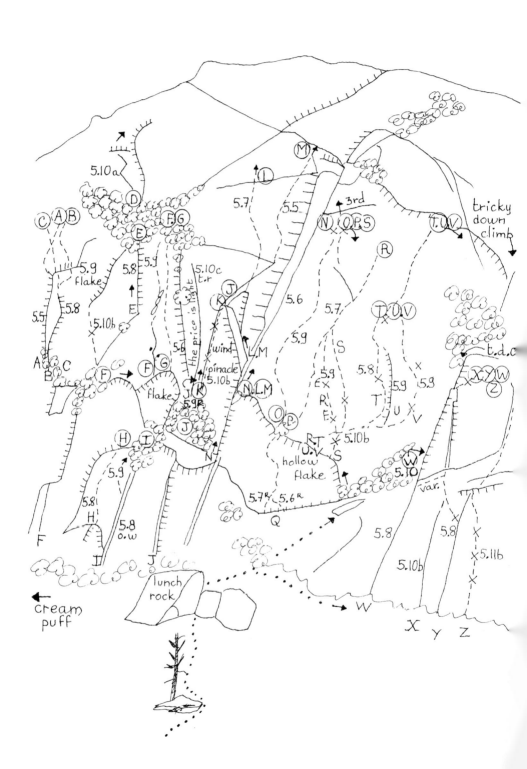

THE PIE SHOP — West

A **The Saw** 5.5
B **Fear of Flying** 5.9
C **Archer** 5.8
D **Zig Zag Finish** 5.10a
E **Clean Corner** 5.8
F **B.T. Express** 5.9 pro: to 2"
G **Short Cake** 5.6 pro: slings
H **Cruise Control** 5.8
I **Mad Wife** 5.8
J **Shelob's Lair** 5.9 R pro: to 4"
K **Wind** 5.10b
L **Knobhill** 5.7 pro: slings
M **Fluted Crust** 5.5 pro: to 2"

N **Crepes Corner** 5.7 pro: to 2½"
O **Earn Your Wings** 5.9
P **Pie in the Sky** 5.7 pro: small
Q **Direct Starts** 5.6/5.7 R
R **Miller's Highlife** 5.9
S **Teenage Wasteland** 5.10b
T **Headjammer** 5.8 pro: slings
U **Pie Face Dihedral** 5.9
V **Head East** 5.9
W **Deliverance** 5.10 pro: to 4"
X **Desiderata** 5.10b pro: to 1½"
Y **Hands Masseuse** 5.8 pro: to 3"
Z **The Last Dance** 5.11b

THE CREAM PUFF

The Cream Puff is a free-standing pinnacle located 100 yards uphill from **Archer,** at the far west end of the Pie Shop face. It is about 70 feet high on its south and west sides, where the following routes are located.

Cream Puff 60', 5.7 pro: to 3½"
On the west side of the pinnacle is a strenuous diagonal crack that leads to a short face.

7-11 Cracks 5.8, 5.10c, 5.10c pro: RP's
On the south side of the Cream Puff are three prominent cracks, all ending at the overhanging summit block. The left crack is 5.8. The middle crack starts with a steep 5.10b lieback which soon widens to allow fist jams. At this point move right onto the face to a flake. Load this flake with RP's to protect a 5.10 face lunge to bigger holds and the summit block. The right hand crack is an awkward leaning affair with hard-to-obtain protection. The overhang is surmounted via a wild but moderate hand traverse and mantle, then easy face leads to the top.

Descent. A bolt offers a short rappel, or one can down climb 4th class (scary and loose) to the east.

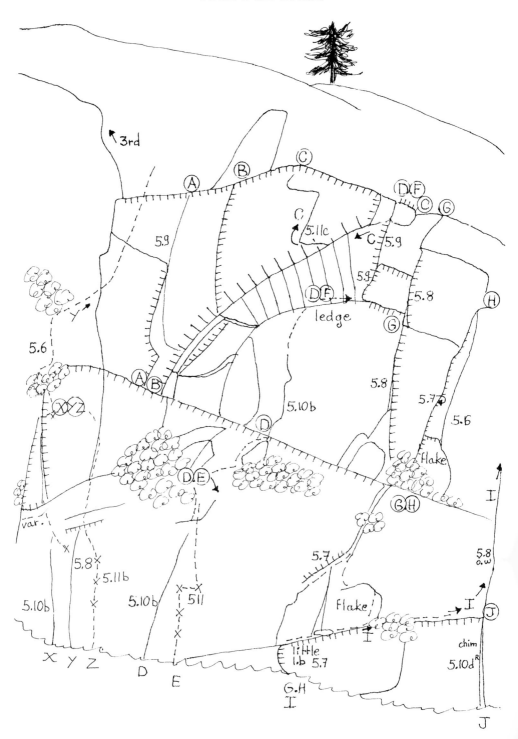

THE PIE SHOP — Center

X Desiderata 5.10b pro: to 1½"
Y Hands Masseuse 5.8 pro: to 3"
Z The Last Dance 5.11b
A The Hermit 5.9
B Ancient Route 5.7
C Natural High (Blood in my Chalkbag) 5.11c
D True Grip 5.10b pro: to 2"
E Poly Grip 5.11
F Mincemeat Variation 5.9
G The Slot 5.8 pro: to 3"
H Humble Pie 5.7
I Hindsight 5.8
J Dropout 5.10d R pro: to 2½"

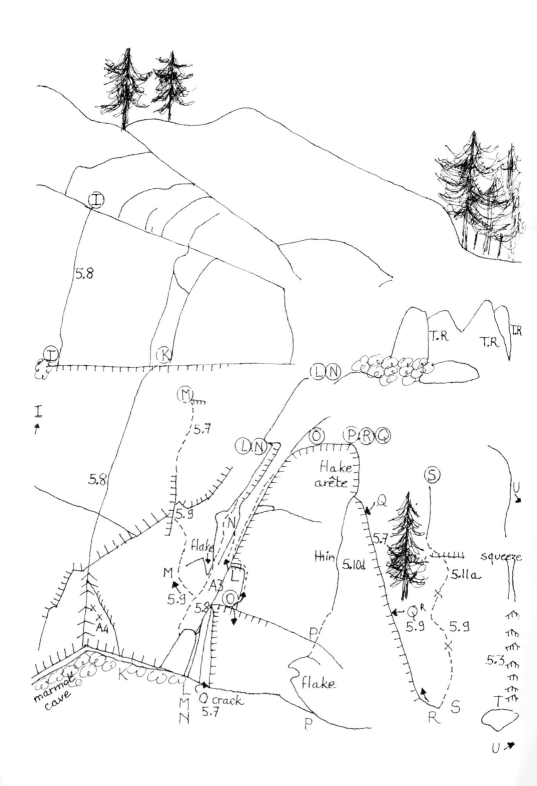

5.8

T.R

T.R

T.R

5.8

I
↑

M
5.7

L N

O   P R Q

Flake
arête

S

U

5.9

N

Q

5.7

flake

Thin   5.10d

squeeze

M

5.11a

5.9   A3   L

O

M
N

A4

5.8

Q R
5.9   5.9

P

5.3

marmot
cave

K

P

flake

T

L
M
N

O crack
5.7

P

R   S

U →

THE PIE SHOP — East

I Hindsight 5.8

K Marmot Pie 5.8 A4   pro: 15 thin pitons, nuts to 2", skyhooks

L Moss Pie 5.8   pro: to 3"

M Hair Pie 5.9   pro: to 2"

N The Walrus 5.8 A3   pro: thin pitons to 1", nuts to 2"

O Ambrosia 5.7   pro: to 2½"

P Altair 5.10d   pro: to 3"

Q No Future 5.9 R

R J Walk 5.7   pro: to 2½"

S Wipeout 5.11a   pro: thin stoppers, ½" web. slings

T Burnt Pie 5.3   pro: to 2"

U Simple Simon 5.2   The arch right of the pillar. pro: to 2"

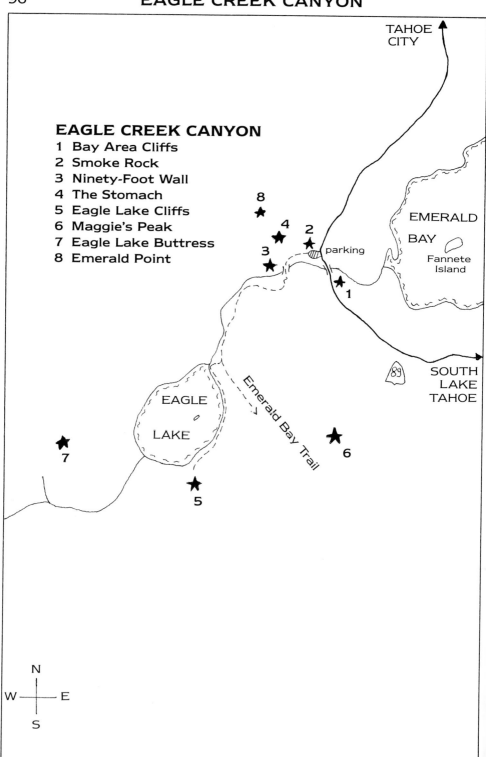

EAGLE CREEK CANYON
1 Bay Area Cliffs
2 Smoke Rock
3 Ninety-Foot Wall
4 The Stomach
5 Eagle Lake Cliffs
6 Maggie's Peak
7 Eagle Lake Buttress
8 Emerald Point

EAGLE CREEK CANYON

Along the West Shore of Lake Tahoe on Highway 89 is Emerald Bay. Directly above the bay on the west side of the highway is a parking lot for the trailhead up Eagle Creek Canyon and into the Desolation Wilderness. Smoke Rock, a big boulder, is about 100 yards north of the parking lot. The Bay Area Cliffs are located below the road, overlooking Emerald Bay.

Eagle Creek Canyon leads west above Emerald Bay and offers a multitude of small cliffs and spires in an alpine setting. Ninety-Foot Wall lies within ½ mile of the parking lot on the north side of the creek, and Eagle Lake Cliffs rise above the south shore of Eagle Lake, about two miles from the trailhead. The trail is well marked, and it is possible to camp along the south shore of Eagle Lake provided that you have a wilderness permit. This permit is easily obtained at no charge from any U.S. Forest Service office in South Lake Tahoe. Eagle Lake Buttress looks down from high above the north shore of Eagle Lake; one can reach its base by scrambling for a half mile up steep slopes and gullies. The broken northwest face of Maggie's Peak rises near the junction of the Eagle Lake and Velma Lakes trails. Westward up the Velma Lakes trail one can find numerous short but exciting clifflets and extensive bouldering. Finally, rising over 1500 feet above the north side of the canyon and extending nearly two miles from the highway to Grouse Lake Valley is the enormous and complex exposure of Emerald Point. Though serious bushwacking is necessary to reach these cliffs, there are many first ascent possibilities here to reward the adventuresome and energetic.

The Emerald Bay/Eagle Creek area is very popular among tourists and hikers as well as climbers. During the warm season it can be very crowded; therefore, the usual cautions should be observed. Giardia is an ever-present possibility, so the water should be treated accordingly. And, unfortunately, there have been instances of theft from the parking lot, so it is recommended that you do not leave any valuables in your car.

The following areas are listed in the order in which they appear as one travels west up the canyon.

BAY AREA CLIFFS

The Bay Area Cliffs can be found by walking about 50 yards up the road from the entrance to the parking area and descending about 150 yards down an ill-defined gully/trail toward the bay. The small, east facing cliffs will appear on the left. The cliff is marked by a right facing corner and, further to the right, three parallel overhanging cracks. There is a good bolt anchor at the top of the widest crack. There are about ten quality routes on good granite, all approximately 70 feet long, ranging in difficulty from 5.6 to 5.11+.

SMOKE ROCK

Smoke Rock is a large smoke-blackened boulder lying about 100 yards north of the parking area. It is 50 feet high and gently overhanging. One can find several fine cracks ranging from 5.8 to 5.11. Bolts on top provide good top-rope anchors.

NINETY-FOOT WALL

Ninety-Foot Wall is a steep cliff of solid and dark granite, laced with cracks and seams and dotted with small, square-cut holds. Its actual height is closer to 70 feet than 90 feet, and all the routes can be top roped with a 165 foot rope.

To reach the crag, walk up the Eagle Lake trail from the parking lot until coming to a bridge across the creek. Stay on the right side of the water and continue upstream for 50 yards; the cliff can then be seen about 25 yards up a slope to the right. An alternative approach is to branch off the trail about 50 yards before the bridge, angling up right and over a small ridge. Walking west leads directly to the base of the wall.

This cliff is very popular and can be crowded, especially on weekends. The climbs are of excellent quality and though they are most frequently top roped, almost all of them have been led. Bolts and natural features on top provide good top rope anchors, but long slings (and nuts for back ups) are necessary. The easiest approach to and descent from the top is found on the west end of the trail, up a gentle gully.

THE STOMACH

This aptly named formation is a whitish granite dome about 500 feet above and east of the Ninety-Foot Wall. To reach its base walk up ledges and terraces for several hundred feet above the Ninety-Foot Wall to a big pine tree. Bushwhacking is necessary from this point to reach the base of the rock, 50 yards away. There are only a few routes here, mostly easy ones, and one 5.9 top rope problem. The poor protection and bushwhacking have much to do with the lack of development.

NINETY-FOOT WALL   photo: Bill Serniuk

EAGLE CREEK CANYON

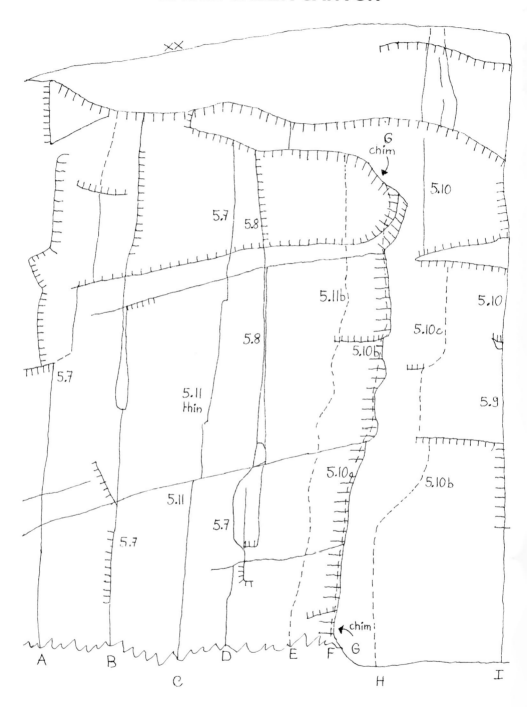

NINETY-FOOT WALL — West Side

A Shuman the Human 5.7
B Rentier 5.7
C Lost in Space 5.11a
D Strontium 90 5.8
E Bastille 5.11b
F Relativity 5.10b
G Casual Observer 5.1
H Alias Emil Bart 5.10c
I Ripoff 5.10

NINETY-FOOT WALL — Middle
I Ripoff 5.10
J Never Ending Story 5.11
K Fallout 5.9
L Holdless Horror 5.6
M Bachar's Line 5.11
N Vintage 85 5.9
O Lightning Bolt 5.10b

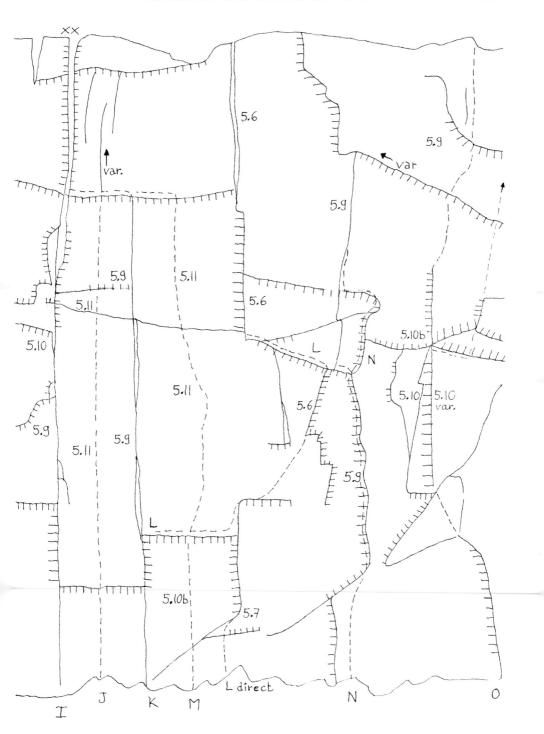

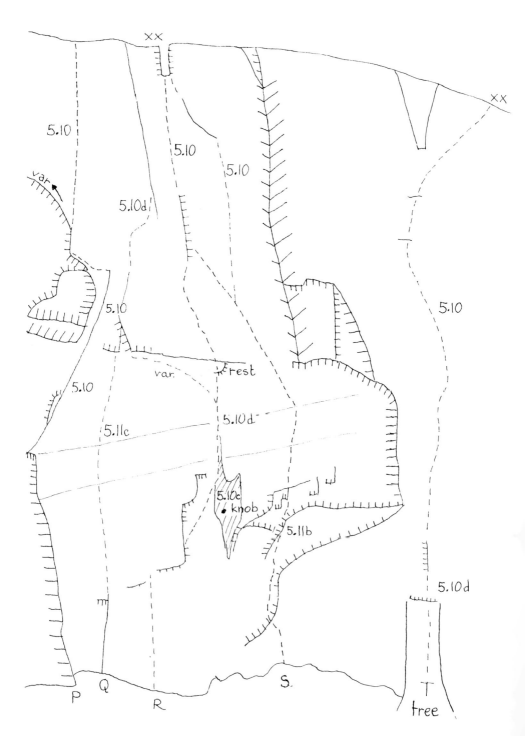

NINETY-FOOT WALL — East

P Ice Nine 5.10a
Q Polar Circus 5.11c
R Ti-si-ack 5.10d
S Dave's Run 5.11b
T One More for the Road 5.10d

There is an infinite number of variations to these problems; virtually every inch of this rock has been climbed.

EAGLE LAKE CLIFFS

Above the south corner of Eagle Lake, on either side of the incoming creek, are granite cliffs which extend ¼ mile upstream. These cliffs are up to 200 feet in height and have an average 95° steepness. The quality, severity, and good protection make the climbs here well worth the long walk. To reach them, hike up the trail to Eagle Lake, continue around the south shore of the lake, then go up a small talus slope to the base of the cliffs. Most of the climbs are on the south side of the creek, although one can cross over and find a few shorter routes on the north side. To descend from the south side cliffs walk south to gullies, ramps and bushes, then descend 3rd class to the lake.

MAGGIE'S PEAK

The northwest face of Maggie's Peak is an 800 foot broken and terraced cliff rising to the southeast of Eagle Lake. This face is not very popular with the local climbers, mostly because the rock can be poor or badly fractured in places. However, some fine routes have been done, ranging from 5.8 to 5.11, and some intriguing crack systems await first ascents from those with good route finding skills. Some of the best ice climbing in the Tahoe Basin can be found in the north facing gullies of this peak when the weather conditions are favorable for the formation of good ice.

To get to Maggie's, hike up the Eagle Lake Trail to the junction of Eagle Lake and Velma Lakes trails. (There is a sign post.) Take the left fork and continue up the Velma Lakes trail for ¼ mile; the cliff will become visible up to the left. Some scrambling and 3rd class is necessary to reach the base. To descend from the upper wall, traverse west on ledges and terraces to a long and narrow talus slope that forms the western boundary of the face. Descend this talus slope to the trail.

EAGLE LAKE CLIFFS
A The Criterion 5.11a
B Thrust is a Must 5.10d pro: to 3", mainly medium
C The Nagual 5.10c pro: to 2½"
D Seams to Me 5.10c pro: thin to 1½"

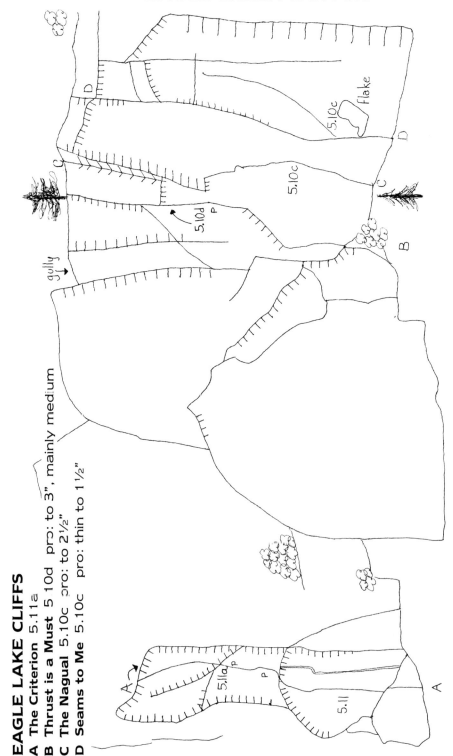

photo: Christine Jenkewitz-Meytras

EAGLE LAKE CLIFFS

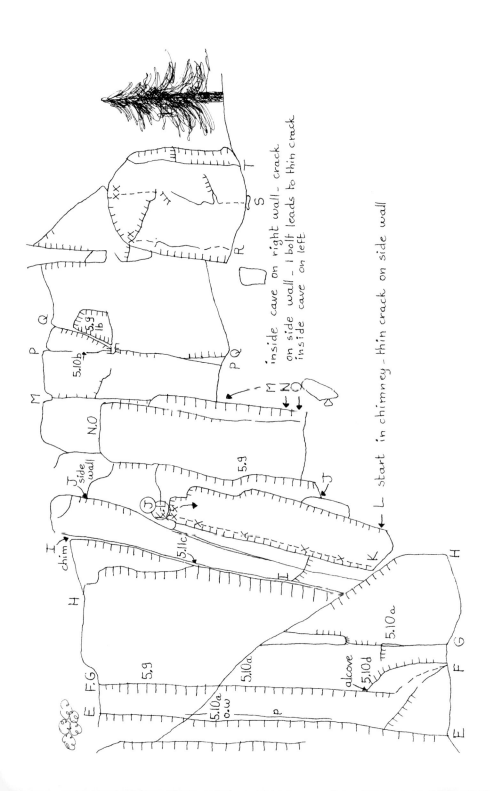

M   inside cave on right wall - crack
      on side wall - 1 bolt leads to thin crack
      inside cave on left

L   start in chimney - thin crack on side wall

EAGLE LAKE CLIFFS
E Barney Rubble 5.10a
F Quest for Glory 5.10d
G Space Truckin' 5.10a   pro: to 2½", mainly medium
H Space Walk 5.11c/d   pro: to 2", mainly small to medium
I Separated Reality 5.8
J The Vulture 5.10a
K Off the Wall 5.10b
L Polecat A3 pro: many thin horizontals
M Cracula 5.10a pro: to 2"
N The Buzzard 5.11b
O Changeling 5.8
P Buster Brown 5.10b pro: to 4"
Q Block Buster 5.9 pro: to 3½"
R Master Race 5.11c top rope
S Der Führer 5.11d top rope
T Master of Disaster 5.10a

THREE STOOGES WALL (or Pep Boys Crag)
Three Stooges Wall is found on a flat rock plateau high above the southwest shore of Eagle Lake. Follow the Eagle Lake trail, take the Velma Lakes fork, and continue up past Maggie's Peak for about another mile, which brings one to the plateau. Walk west across the plateau to the rock wall, which is slightly hidden behind pine trees. At the right end of the wall are the following three short overhanging cracks. Other climbs have been done to the right, around the corner, and many new lines can be found in this largely unmapped area.

The Manny 5.12
This is the thin crack on the left side.
The MO Crack 5.10a
This is the center crack.
The Jack Crack 5.10d
This is the right crack.

PUNK ROCK
Punk Rock is up and right of Eagle Lake Cliffs. It is a small cliff with a thin, right leaning flake in the center. Three routes have been established: **Lost and Found**, 5.9, climbs up the flake; **Atomic Punk**, 5.10c, a corner and roof on the right side of the cliff; and **Moon Raker**, 5.10a, which follows an obvious left facing corner on the left side of the rock.

UPPER EAGLE LAKE CLIFFS

From the base of Eagle Lake Cliffs more cliff bands can be seen extending west up the canyon and on either side of the creek. Many fine climbs have been done here. The rock is of good quality and the routes range from 5.9 to 5.11d or 5.12. One of the best routes of the area:

Gold Mettle 5.11d or 5.12a   pro: Friends and stoppers
On the right side of the canyon west of Eagle Lake Cliffs is a bulging gold-colored wall split by a 2-4" crack. No cheat stones allowed.

EAGLE LAKE BUTTRESS

Eagle Lake Buttress is a very fine granite tower that rises to 8640 feet at the south end fo a long and high ridge a mile west of Eagle Lake. Two hours of hiking are required from the parking lot at Emerald Bay.

To reach the base of the tower, cross the outlet at Eagle Lake and hike up a ravine and a slabby area on the right. Attain a ridge and follow it to the base of the buttress.

This pyramid-shaped formation offers some of the best granite in the canyon, magnificent views and warm rock due to the sunny southern exposure. Fine bivouac sites can be found at the base of the south face. However, because of the long approach march, this fine climbing area is seldom visited.

The easiest descent from the summit goes down the **Mountaineer's Route:** a short 4th class slab just beneath the summit is down climbed to easier terrain.

The following routes are described from left to right, beginning at the southwest corner.

Mountaineer's Route 4th class
Scramble up lower angle slabs from the southwest corner of the rock (3rd class). Steep slabs are climbed (4th class) to a notch between Eagle Lake Buttress and a subsidiary pinnacle on its west side. Follow the ridge to the top.

A Line 40', 5.9   pro: to 2½"
Seen from below and right of the buttress, this route follows the obvious left leaning crack system to the top. The first pitch is about 100 feet long; the first half is 4th class, the second half passes two roofs (5.8) to a small ledge via a jam crack. Climb straight up, passing another ceiling (5.7). Climb low angle slabs to a large belay ledge below an intimidating bulge. An offwidth crack (5.9) leads over the bulge, and a long jam crack (5.8) leads for 100 feet to a small ledge on the left. Mantle up right (5.8) and follow an easy gully to the top.

EAGLE LAKE BUTTRESS
A Mountaineer's Route 4th class
B A Line 5.9
C I'm Gunby Dummit 5.9
D Wind Tree 5.9
E Eagle Route 5.5
F Monkey Business 5.10a
G Orange Book 5.8
H Orange Sunshine 5.9
I East Ridge Route 5.7

photo: Christine Jenkewitz-Meytras

I'm Gunby Dummit 440', 5.9
Climb an overhanging crack just to the right of the start of the **A Line.** There is one hard move at the top of the pitch. Belay at the base of a perfect 60 foot corner. Climb to the top of the corner. Step across a ramp to a thin crack and continue to the top.

Wind Tree 380', 5.9   pro: to 3"
High on the backbone of the buttress stands a lone, windblown juniper: the Wind Tree. This route follows an obvious left leaning crack system to the tree. Several 3rd class variations lead to a ledge 40 feet above the ground. Rope up and climb broken cracks to a small ledge where two cracks form a prominent "V". Follow the left crack, a right facing corner. Seventy-five feet of moderate climbing ends at a large belay ledge. Overcome a steep section. Follow a big arch until a vegetated dihedral is almost reached. Move right on knobs to follow a difficult (5.9) fist and offwidth crack. Climb up and right to the Wind Tree. Traverse straight left to an arête and jam strenuous leaning cracks (5.9) to much easier climbing and the summit.

Eagle Route 275', 5.5
This route follows the right side of the prominent "V" on the south face mentioned in the **Wind Tree** description. Climb the **Wind Tree** route to the small ledge at the base of the "V." Follow a straight-in crack on the right to a large sloping belay ledge. A similar pitch leads up cracks to a belay just above a groove. Move left to a flared chimney containing a flake. Follow the **East Ridge Route** to the top.

Monkey Business 350', 5.10a   pro: to 2½", mainly small
This superb route lies in the center of an obscure buttress just left of the **Orange Book.** A big juniper at the base of the rock marks the rope-up spot. Climb a short jam crack (5.7) and chimney to a long broken gully. Continue to a large belay area just a few feet left of the **Orange Book.** The next pitch ascends the triangular overhang directly above A short jam and strenuous lieback (5.9, poor protection) leads up under the right side of the overhang. Make a gymnastic move left to enter a wide crack that passes over the lip of the overhang. Take a thin finger crack (5.8) up and right above the overhang. Climb ramps back left to a small ledge on the exposed arête. From the belay follow a jam crack (5.8) that splits the center of the arête. Climb lower angle rock to the **East Ridge,** following that route to the top.

Orange Book 5.8
This route follows the most prominent feature on the buttress, a large left facing orange dihedral. Stem and jam (5.7) up the corner for 90 feet to a good ledge. Continue up the corner (5.5) to a belay where the corner begins to overhang. Climb difficult cracks (5.8) and chimneys through the overhangs to the **East Ridge,** and follow

that route to the top. **Variation** 5.6 From the top of the second pitch drop down and right to a hole. Slide through the hole to a short lieback (5.6) in a steepening corner. Shortly thereafter the **East Ridge** is reached.

Orange Sunshine 260', 5.9   pro: to 2½"

On the right hand sidewall of **Orange Book** one can see a pair of thin vertical cracks that begin about 120 feet above the ground. Climb the first pitch of **Orange Book** to a belay ledge directly below the cracks. Move up and right, pass an overhang (5.8), then jam and lieback the left hand crack (5.9). Belay on "King Henry," a broken terrace on the East Ridge. Follow the **East Ridge Route** to the top.

East Ridge Route 370', 5.7   pro: to 2"

This is probably the most scenic route on the buttress, with beautiful views of Eagle Creek Canyon and the pinnacled ridge that stretches northwest from the buttress. Ascend slabs and easy rocks on the north side of the ridge to a ledge at the base of a steep crack. A short, curving crack leads to the main crack which is followed to sloping ledges. Move right and climb steep rock (5.7) to Bay View Terrace, an excellent belay platform on the prow of the ridge. Several difficult cracks rise in the wall above, the easiest being the rightmost of a pair of wide cracks. Belay above on a broken terrace known as "King Henry." Jam a curving crack (5.7) and scramble up blocks until the ridge turns into 3rd class. Follow the ridge on low angle rock to the final steep summit wall. 5.5 cracks lead to the top.

EMERALD POINT

At 9195 feet, Emerald Point is the second highest peak on the Rubicon Crest. Its giant southern face borders Eagle Creek Canyon for nearly two miles upstream from the highway. It is a complicated mountain, showing a confusion of intersecting ridges, gullies and terraces, and its base is guarded by thick brush. The crag is not very well explored, mostly because of the steep and brushy approach. However, the existing routes offer varied and interesting climbing on mixed granite that improves with altitude. The best approach to the established routes is by following Eagle Creek up past the Ninety-Foot Wall for another ½ mile until reaching a huge round boulder at the bottom of a shallow ravine that extends up toward the peak. A short distance up the right side of the ravine is a talus field that leads to the base of the rock near a huge white dihedral: the "White Walls."

Emerald Point offers many first ascent possibilities and several good routes ranging from 5.7 to 5.9 and A1, the most popular of these being **Section 20,** a long and varied 5.7 route. The easiest descent from the top is by following the west ridge down (3rd class) until it is possible to descend a long narrow gully toward the creek.

THE PLECTRUM

The Plectrum is the sharpest and most spectacular of several pinnacles on the summit ridge of Emerald Point. It rises within 50 yards of the top of **Section 20.** The best way to reach the pinnacle is to first climb **Section 20,** then traverse eastward along the ridge. Several routes have been climbed here, all about 250 feet long, ranging from 5.6 A1 to 5.9.

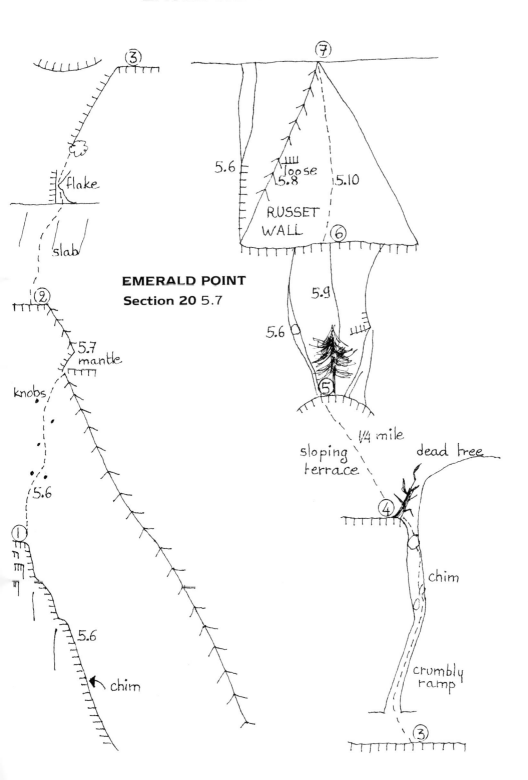

EMERALD POINT
Section 20 5.7

DONNER SUMMIT

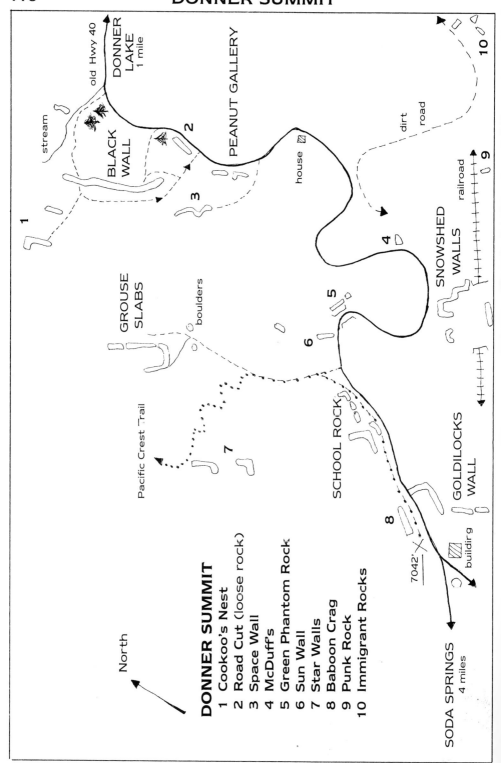

North

DONNER SUMMIT

1 Cookoo's Nest
2 Road Cut (loose rock)
3 Space Wall
4 McDuff's
5 Green Phantom Rock
6 Sun Wall
7 Star Walls
8 Baboon Crag
9 Punk Rock
10 Immigrant Rocks

old Hwy 40

DONNER LAKE
1 mile

stream

BLACK WALL

PEANUT GALLERY

house

dirt road

railroad

SNOWSHED WALLS

GROUSE SLABS

boulders

Pacific Crest Trail

SCHOOL ROCK

GOLDILOCKS WALL

7042'

building

SODA SPRINGS
4 miles

DONNER SUMMIT

The climbing area known as Donner Summit lies alongside old Highway 40, once the major link between the east and west sides of the Sierra Nevada. With the completion of Interstate 80, the old winding road now sees mostly local use, a fact which should delight all climbers who play there.

Numerous crags dot the landscape. None are so impressive or spectacular as to raise many eyebrows. These climbs must be experienced to be fully appreciated. Perhaps for this very reason the area has only recently been "discovered" by outsiders.

The crags and routes depicted in these topos are but a sampling of the area's delights. Other crags are listed by number in the overview map of the area. Three other areas nearby deserve at least mention. One is "Rainbow," located about eight miles to the west down Interstate 80. Another group of crags, the "Freeway Crags," lie close to Interstate 80, in a line with the main Donner Summit crags. "River Rock," another crag, is located by Interstate 80 about half-way between Truckee and Reno. Check with the locals, either at the crags or at the local shops, for further information about these areas.

GENE DRAKE

BLACK WALL

There are two easy ways to reach Black Wall from the road. Both ways involve about 10 to 15 minutes of hiking and virtually no bushwhacking.

The first approach leads to a small cliff with a tall prominent pine tree. Pass the cliff on the right and head more or less straight up through a boulderfield to the base of Black Wall in the vicinity of the **Rat's Tooth.**

The other approach leads to the routes at the far right, such as **Rated X.** Scramble up toward another tall pine tree. Walk up slabs, then follow a streambed (usually active until late June). Look for a faint trail that heads toward the wall (**The Labyrinth**), then veers left along its base.

The normal descent from the top of the Black Wall follows a faint trail to the southeast and reaches the road just above the roadcut. Some climbers prefer leaving a pack at the base of Black Wall and may wish to do more climbing there as well. They should follow the previous descent description a short way, then traverse left to the southeast ridge. Easy hiking but tricky route finding leads across to the top of the "Primer Boulder."

BLACK WALL

A **Cannibal Gully** 5.7
B **Rat's Tooth** 5.10a
C **Hungover-Hangover** 5.10a
D **Empty Sky** 5.10a
E **Touch and Go** 5.9
F **Pinball Junkie** 5.11a
G **Bourbon Street** 5.10a
H **Bliss** 5.10d
I **Fascination** 5.10c
J **Space Invaders** 5.10b

Empty Cargo 5.10a
This is a combination of **B, C, D**

PRIMER BOULDER

Last Tango 5.11c   thin crack
Primer 5.9   green corner
Delusions of Desperation 5.10a   nuts to 2", mostly tiny and small
Climb a crack, then go right across a face to a thin flake system. A direct variation (5.10+) that follows tiny face holds has been done on a top rope.

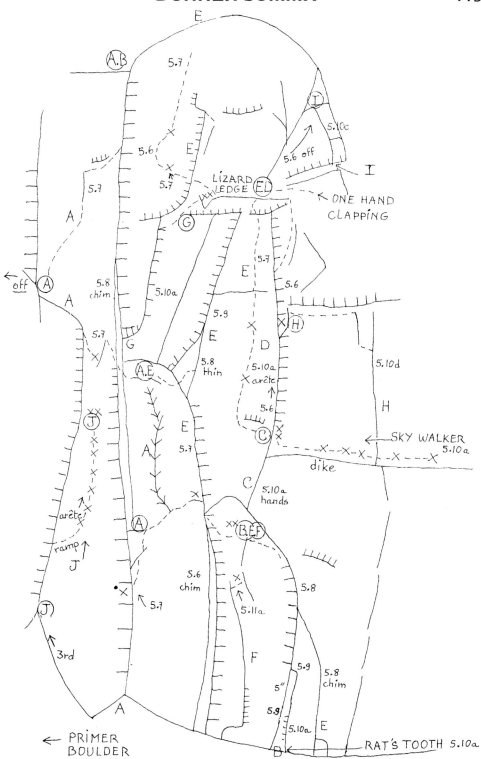

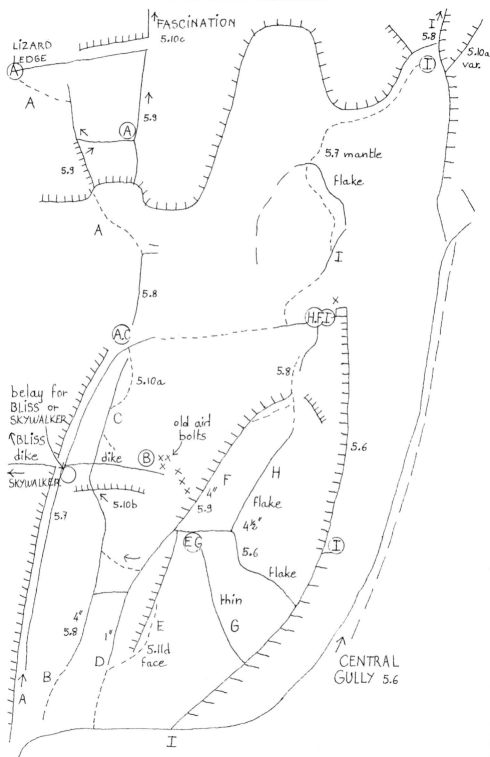

BLACK WALL
A One Hand Clapping 5.9
B Firecracker 5.10b
C Tiptoe 5.10a
D New Moon 5.10d
E Full Moon 5.11d
F Moonshine 5.9
G Future Games 5.10b
H Aqualung 5.10c
I On Ramp 5.8

New Fascination 5.10d
This is a combination of **D, B, C, A,** and **Fascination.**

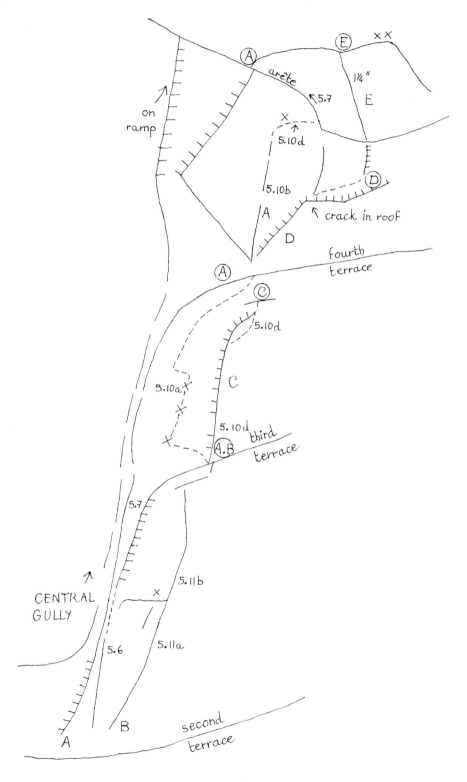

BLACK WALL
A Next 5.10d
B Slipstream 5.11b
C No Stems-No Seeds 5.10d
D Sky Pilot 5.11c
E Headstone 5.11b

Imaginary Voyage 5.11c
This is a combination of **B, C, D, and E.**

BLACK WALL
A The Fuse 5.10c
B Mr. Clean 5.10c/d
C Inside Out 5.8
D Protection Difficult 5.8
E Give Me Slack 5.7
F Super Slab 5.10a
G Donner Delight 5.8
H Silver Book 5.7
I Tilt 5.10a
J Full Tilt 5.11a
K Voyeur 5.9

Cucumber Slumber 5.10b
Start from the third terrace, next to the **Porno Book.** Follow a zig-
zagging crack up a vertical wall, the right side of the **Porno Book.**

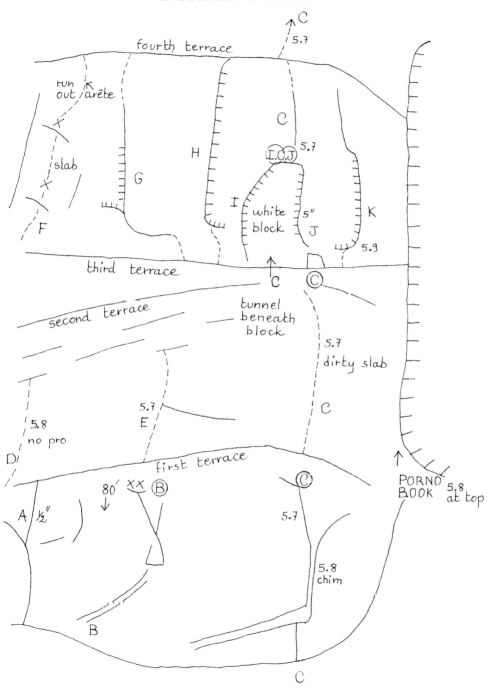

photo: Harvey Overland

THE BLACK WALL

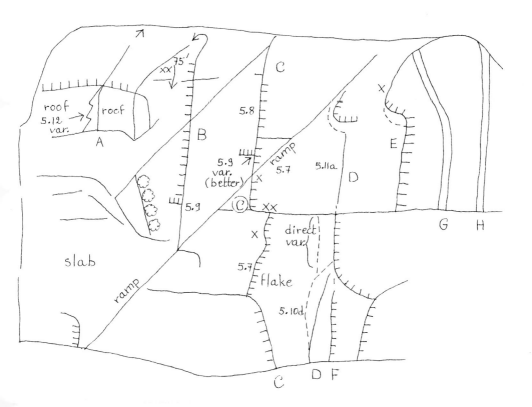

BLACK WALL
A Lightning Bolt Roof 5.11a
B Black September 5.9
C Rated X 5.8 (5.9)
D Fingerlicker 5.11a   hard work to protect first pitch
E The Hook 5.11d top rope
F Bridwell's Climb 5.11a
G Labyrinth 5.6

PEANUT GALLERY   photo: Harvey Overland

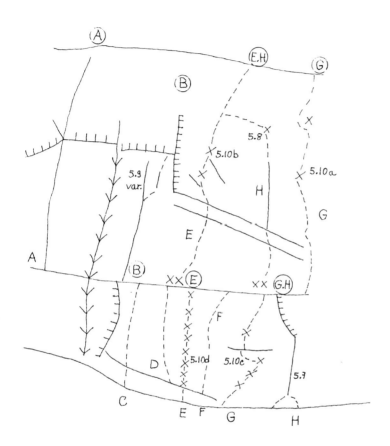

PEANUT GALLERY — Southeast Face
A Shoot Out 5.8
B Change Up 5.8
C Scratchin' Nails 5.10b top rope (has been soloed)
D Finger Graffitti 5.11c top rope
E Bolt Run 5.10d
F 5.11a top rope
G Eyes of Silver 5.10c
H Middle Ages 5.8

Jack of Hearts 5.10a   pro: a few nuts to 1½"
Three bolts protect the face around the corner from the second pitch of **Eyes of Silver.**
Bluff 5.7
Crack system just to the right of **Jack of Hearts.**

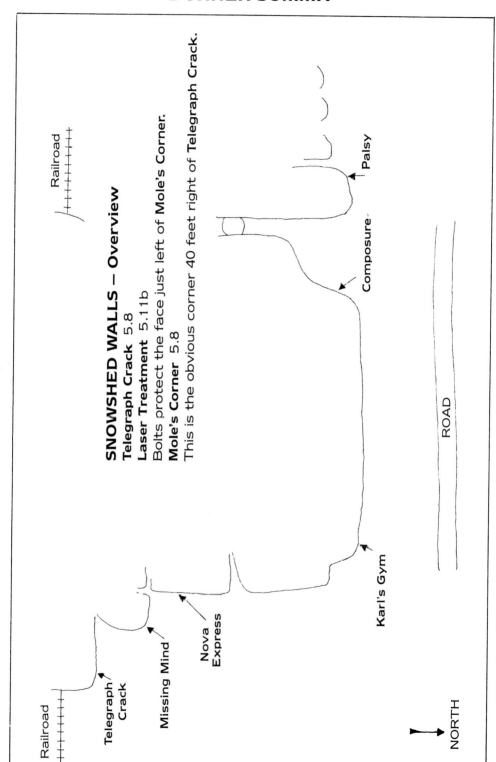

Railroad

Railroad

SNOWSHED WALLS – Overview

Telegraph Crack 5.8

Laser Treatment 5.11b
Bolts protect the face just left of Mole's Corner.

Mole's Corner 5.8
This is the obvious corner 40 feet right of Telegraph Crack.

Palsy

Composure

Karl's Gym

Nova
Express

Missing Mind

Telegraph
Crack

ROAD

NORTH

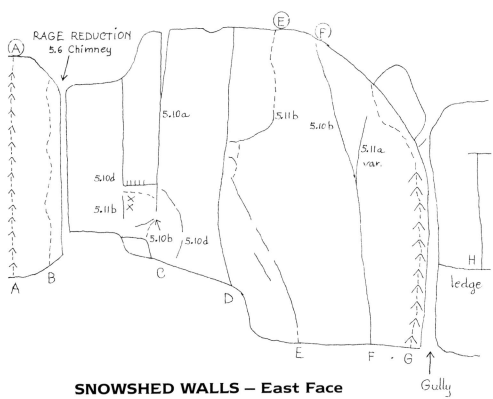

SNOWSHED WALLS — East Face

A Missing Mind 5.11c top rope
B Brain Child 5.12 top rope
C Dropouts 5.10b-5.11b
D Nova Express 5.9
E Welcome to My Nightmare 5.11b   serious
F Farewell to Arms 5.10b
G Little Feat 5.10d   serious
H Sanitation Crack 5.10c

CLIMBS IN GULLY (left of Sanitation Crack)
Night Gallery 5.10b
This is the obvious crack on left wall of the gully.
Side Effect 5.9
A steep corner on the right wall.
Night Country 5.11b
The thin crack on the right wall.

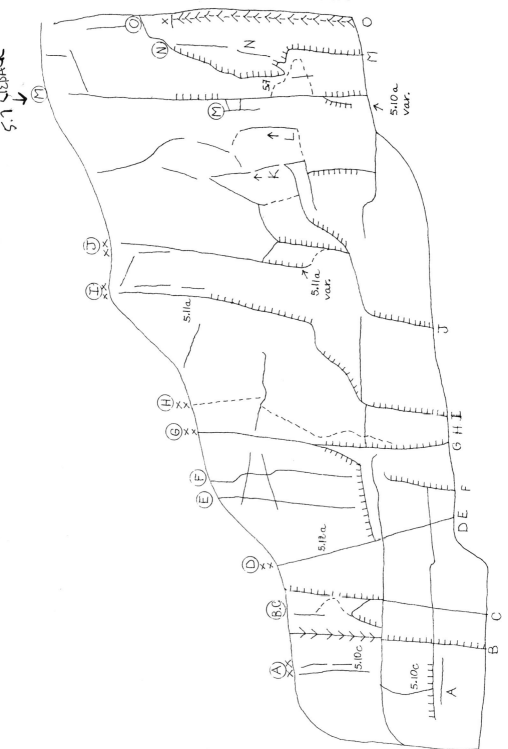

SNOWSHED WALLS – North Face

A Karl's Gym 5.10d
B Split Pea 5.8
C Pea Soup 5.9 (60')
D Bell Bottom Blues 5.12a
E Manic Depression 5.11c
F Monkey Paws 5.12a
G Bottomless-Topless 5.10a (75')
H Panic in Detroit 5.12c
I Peter Principle 5.11a
J The Thing 5.10d
K The Boys are Back 5.11c top rope
L Seems to Me 5.11d top rope
M Devaluation 5.7
N Crack of the Eighties 5.12d
O Aerial 5.11b top rope

Bertha Butt Boogie 5.10c
Climb a slanting crack (5.10a) around the corner (left) from Karl's Gym. The final crack (5.10c) leads to face climbing and ends at bolts also used by Karl's Gym

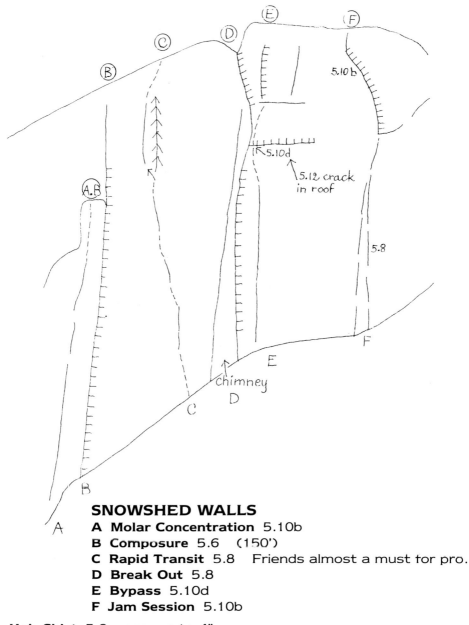

SNOWSHED WALLS
A **Molar Concentration** 5.10b
B **Composure** 5.6 (150')
C **Rapid Transit** 5.8 Friends almost a must for pro.
D **Break Out** 5.8
E **Bypass** 5.10d
F **Jam Session** 5.10b

Hair Shirt 5.8 pro. up to 4"
The buttress right of the gully has two parallel cracks. This route goes up the left crack.
Palsy 5.9
This is the right crack. Start (5.9) in the gully right of the buttress. A direct start is 5.10b, on the north face.

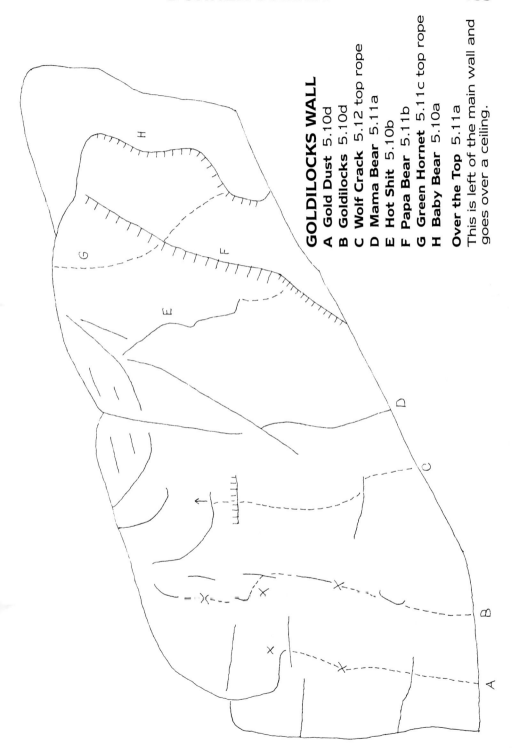

GOLDILOCKS WALL

A Gold Dust 5.10d
B Goldilocks 5.10d
C Wolf Crack 5.12 top rope
D Mama Bear 5.11a
E Hot Shit 5.10b
F Papa Bear 5.11b
G Green Hornet 5.11c top rope
H Baby Bear 5.10a

Over the Top 5.11a
This is left of the main wall and goes over a ceiling.

photo: Harvey Overland

SCHOOL ROCK — South Face
A Kindergarten Crack 5.5-5.6
B Mary's Crack 5.8
C Junior High 5.6

Karl's Overhang 5.11a
This route climbs a hand crack in a ceiling at the far right side of the cliff, just above the ground and near a boulder.
Teacher's Pet 5.10b   pro: up to 3"
This is the second crack left of **Eleventh Grade Corner**, on the east face of the rock. Follow a crack up and right until it is possible to traverse left to a better crack. This route has a bolt which is no longer needed, due to modern protection.
Senior Prom 5.9
This is the crack system just left of **Eleventh Grade Corner**. What appears at first to be a dirty climb turns out to be a great one.
Eleventh Grade Corner 5.8
An old classic.

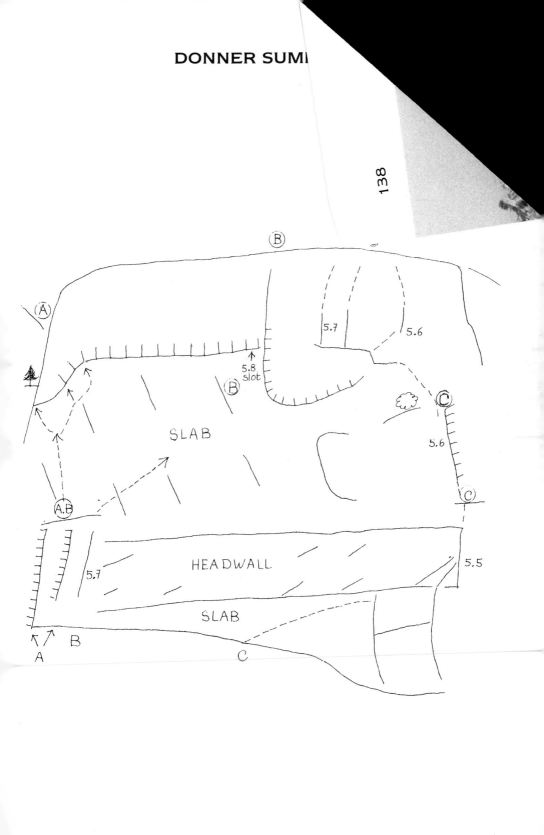

DONNER SUMMIT

Mitigate

Jelly Roll Arch

Slow Hand

GROUSE SLABS   photo: Harvey Overland

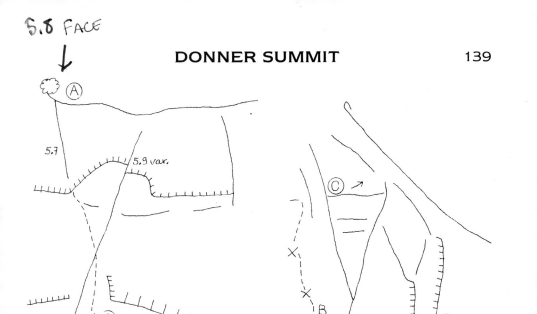

5.8 FACE

GROUSE SLABS — East Face
A Jellyroll Arch 5.8   pro: to 2", esp. ¼"-¾"
B Short Cake 5.9
C Insidious 5.6
D Cream Puff 5.10b
E Grease 5.11a

Mitigate 5.7
About 150' right of the previous routes a high point of the talus flows up to the base of the cliff. From there, follow a gully up and slightly left for 150'. The route follows a crack system for two pitches (5.6, 5.7). It ends on the ridge about 150' left of the actual summit.

Slow Hand 5.10d
From the high point of the talus, scramble up and right to a smooth slab capped by a roof. Climb (5.10) to a bolt, then (5.8) up the slab to the roof. Go over the roof (5.10d) via two cracks. Easier rock leads to two bolts.

Pebble in the Sky 5.10a
This is immediately right of **Slow Hand**.

LESSER ROCKS
and CRAGS

INDIAN ROCK

Indian Rock is the largest cliff in the Tahoe Basin. It is located at the northern end of a high rocky ridge that begins at Echo Lakes, and it forms the northwest face of Angora Peak. It is a 1000 foot cliff fractured both horizontally and vertically, and divided by three huge terraces. Between the terraces are sections of excellent granite up to 400 feet in height. All three terraces are accessible via 3rd class scrambling so it is possible to begin climbing from any of the terraces or to retreat from any of them. Indian Rock has dozens of unclimbed crack systems. There are many new route possiblities of high quality and great difficulty, but because of the long approach the cliff is infrequently visited. The existing routes are superb and range from 5.7 to 5.10b A3.

To approach Indian Rock drive on Highway 89 north from the "Y" in South Lake Tahoe. After three miles turn left onto Fallen Leaf Lake Road, and follow the south shore of this lake for a few miles to the resort at its western end. Do not cross the paved bridge over a creek but take the left fork onto a dirt road and continue up to Lily Lake. Park off the road and take the Triangle/Tamarack Lakes Trail for one mile; you will see the long talus slope rising to the southeast to the base of the cliff. Pick your way carefully up this talus since it can be dangerously loose. Allow about one hour from the end of the road. Descend by walking north along any of the terraces.

CRAG PEAK

Crag Peak is located in upper Meeks Creek Canyon and is easily identified by its 400 foot northeast face. The granite is good and steep but lacks well-formed cracks, making protection sometimes difficult to obtain. The routes leading to the notch left of the summit have dangerously loose rock. Because of its 9054 foot elevation and northeast exposure the cliff can be wet from snow melt until mid summer. Several routes have been done, from 5.7 A1 to 5.9, but due to the eight mile approach march from Meeks Bay, Crag Peak is one of the least climbed mountains in the Tahoe Basin.

The best way to reach the base of the cliff is to hike up the Tahoe-Yosemite Trail from Meeks Bay to Hidden Lake, from where Crag Peak comes into view. Hike up a U-shaped valley for a half mile to the base. It is best to plan a campsite at one of the nearby lakes. To descend from the summit, follow the northwest ridge until it becomes possible to cut back and contour the base of the rock.

On rare occasions when ice conditions are very good, an impressive ice climb forms in the main gully/chimney system.

SHAKESPEARE ROCK

This is a 350 foot andesitic plug rising above Highway 50 in Glenbrook. The north face has a multitude of hairline fractures that separate the rock into blocks of all sizes. It lacks well-developed cracks, and the protection is poor. The existing routes are up to 325 feet in height and in the 5.6 range, but there are first ascent possibilities on the hard faces. To get to the climbs, follow a dirt road immediately below the rock on the southeast side of the highway. A steep 300 yard hike leads to the base.

CASTLE ROCK

Castle Rock is a tri-summited formation on the mountainside to the north of Kingsbury Grade (Highway 19). The middle pillar of the south face is over 200 feet high. The rock is coarse and knobby; many of the knobs are friable. The two existing routes are two pitches long and rated 5.8. Descent is down the 30 foot north side.

To reach Castle Rock take Kingsbury Grade up 2½ miles to North Benjamin, turn left and follow this street to Andria; continue on Andria to the end of the pavement. Turn left onto a dirt road and follow this to another dirt road that rises out of the canyon to the west. Follow this to a grassy meadow 100 yards north of the rock.

LUTHER ROCK

Luther Rock is a dark, broken crag located above Highway 89 South in Christmas Valley, three miles southeast of the town of Meyers. It is not a popular crag because the rock is very poor in places and routes are not long. The existing climbs are nonetheless clean and varied on good granite, ranging from 5.7 to 5.10d. The most brush-free approach is a semi-direct line up to the center of the cliff. Care should be taken in the most broken areas, as the rock is very loose. The descent is easily made down either side of the crag.

THE SHIRE

This is also known as Upper Luther Rock since it is on the ridge above and right of Luther Rock. The best way to reach this cliff is to follow Highway 89 south three miles from the junction in Meyers, before turning left onto a little dirt road that starts from a turn-out. Park in an opening in the forest. Bushwhack up and right, then turn up left toward the ridge. Eventually reaching the top of the cliff, descend any gully to the base of the routes. As with Luther Rock, the loose area can be treacherous. To descend, reverse the approach.

WOODFORD'S CANYON

This is a wide rocky canyon that descends east along Highway 88 from Sorenson's Resort. The climbing area starts about two miles east of the Highway 89 junction in Hope Valley, and continues for one mile down the canyon. The walls are high though terraced, and the granite is good. Several climbs have been done here ranging from 5.9 to 5.11c, but the area is not fully explored and numerous first ascents await climbers. The approaches can be long and steep. This area is often climbable in the winter months, as its lower elevation keeps it warmer and dry.

BOULDERI

LOVER'S LEAP — The Boulders

The Boulders of Lover's Leap are located right on the trail below the crag, five minutes from the parking lot. The rock is good, the problems diversified and excellent. It is possible to top rope some of the higher problems.

THE PIE SHOP

Scattered below and around the Pie Shop are numerous boulders offering a wide variety of excellent problems — cracks, faces, overhangs, traverses. These are the most popular boulders in the South Shore. The hardest problems are located near the top of the road that enters Echo View Estates, about a mile down Sawmill Road from Highway 50. Extreme courtesy must be exercised to prevent closure of the area since the boulders are on private land.

EMERALD BAY

The south faces of low granite dome formations can be seen from the road above Eagle Falls, at Emerald Bay. To reach them, walk north on the highway 50 yards past the creek; an indistinct path leads down along the base of the rock. This trail continues down to the Vikingsholm Castle. Located in a sublime setting, the rock is good and the problems many and varied.

D.L. BLISS STATE PARK

Boulders are in abundance throughout the park, located a few miles north of Emerald Bay along Highway 89. The best rocks are found ½ mile south of the park on the lower side of the highway and one mile north of the park at Balanced Rock.

NORTH SHORE BOULDERING

Excellent bouldering is found at Donner Summit. Decent boulders are numerous at the summit, and very good ones can be found in the area of Grouse Slabs. In Truckee, Split Rock, near the entrance of Cold Stream Canyon and at the west end of a small reservoir, offers limited but superb opportunities and is popular with the local climbers. Finally, there is an area called Big Bend/Rainbow about 15 miles west of Truckee, right next to Interstate 80. Check with the locals for more detailed information about these and other North Shore bouldering areas.

OULDERING

y, ½ mile west of the California/Nevada
ay 28 onto Speedway Avenue. Park
and walk down toward the lake. The
st road to the right.

PARK

hway 28, eight miles north of Spooner
th of Incline Village. The boulders are
.... .u uivny the lakeshore, the best ones being found at the
eastern end of the park. Consideration must be given to exposure
and bad (frequently wet) landings.

EAST SHORE

With a little hunting, boulders can be found all along the east
shore of Lake Tahoe, but the finest and most easily reached lie
between Glenbrook and Cave Rock. They can be up to 30 feet in
height, the granite is excellent, and they provide good and varied
problems. One can also find boulders off shore in this area, reachable by boat. This type of bouldering is unusual and very enjoyable.
Girdle traverses run along the base of Cave Rock, just above water
line.

KINGSBURY GRADE

Many boulders stand along both sides of Kingsbury Grade (Highway 19) and along the connecting streets. The best concentration
starts 1½ miles above Highway 50, extends over the summit of
the grade and continues down the other side several miles. The
best rocks on the side streets are on North and South Benjamin
and on Tramway Drive, at the top of the grade. Some of the
boulders are in excess of 40 feet high and may require a belay.

BOULDERING

LOVER'S LEAP — The Boulders
The Boulders of Lover's Leap are located right on the trail below the crag, five minutes from the parking lot. The rock is good, the problems diversified and excellent. It is possible to top rope some of the higher problems.

THE PIE SHOP
Scattered below and around the Pie Shop are numerous boulders offering a wide variety of excellent problems — cracks, faces, overhangs, traverses. These are the most popular boulders in the South Shore. The hardest problems are located near the top of the road that enters Echo View Estates, about a mile down Sawmill Road from Highway 50. Extreme courtesy must be exercised to prevent closure of the area since the boulders are on private land.

EMERALD BAY
The south faces of low granite dome formations can be seen from the road above Eagle Falls, at Emerald Bay. To reach them, walk north on the highway 50 yards past the creek; an indistinct path leads down along the base of the rock. This trail continues down to the Vikingsholm Castle. Located in a sublime setting, the rock is good and the problems many and varied.

D.L. BLISS STATE PARK
Boulders are in abundance throughout the park, located a few miles north of Emerald Bay along Highway 89. The best rocks are found ½ mile south of the park on the lower side of the highway and one mile north of the park at Balanced Rock.

NORTH SHORE BOULDERING
Excellent bouldering is found at Donner Summit. Decent boulders are numerous at the summit, and very good ones can be found in the area of Grouse Slabs. In Truckee, Split Rock, near the entrance of Cold Stream Canyon and at the west end of a small reservoir, offers limited but superb opportunities and is popular with the local climbers. Finally, there is an area called Big Bend/Rainbow about 15 miles west of Truckee, right next to Interstate 80. Check with the locals for more detailed information about these and other North Shore bouldering areas.

SPEEDBOAT AVENUE

This area is near Brockway, ½ mile west of the California/Nevada state line. Turn off Highway 28 onto Speedway Avenue. Park where the road is blocked and walk down toward the lake. The best boulders are off the first road to the right.

SAND HARBOR STATE PARK

This park is located on Highway 28, eight miles north of Spooner Summit and four miles south of Incline Village. The boulders are scattered along the lakeshore, the best ones being found at the eastern end of the park. Consideration must be given to exposure and bad (frequently wet) landings.

EAST SHORE

With a little hunting, boulders can be found all along the east shore of Lake Tahoe, but the finest and most easily reached lie between Glenbrook and Cave Rock. They can be up to 30 feet in height, the granite is excellent, and they provide good and varied problems. One can also find boulders off shore in this area, reachable by boat. This type of bouldering is unusual and very enjoyable. Girdle traverses run along the base of Cave Rock, just above water line.

KINGSBURY GRADE

Many boulders stand along both sides of Kingsbury Grade (Highway 19) and along the connecting streets. The best concentration starts 1½ miles above Highway 50, extends over the summit of the grade and continues down the other side several miles. The best rocks on the side streets are on North and South Benjamin and on Tramway Drive, at the top of the grade. Some of the boulders are in excess of 40 feet high and may require a belay.

TOP ROPING

SPACE INVADERS

This is a huge overhanging 5.12 boulder located on the west side of the Pie Shop, in Echo View Estates. The rock is excellent, and is so overhanging that it affords dry top roping even in the rain. To reach **Space Invaders,** drive north on Sawmill Road until entering Echo View Estates. Turn right on Mount Canary Road and follow it up for two blocks, then turn right and park at the dead end. Walk straight to a gully, then up and right to the base of the rock. It is about a fifteen minute approach.

EMERALD BAY

Emerald Bay offers excellent top roping problems on good quality granite. A small, banded whitish crag — complete with ceilings — lies on the north side of the waterfall and can be approached directly from above. It offers four top rope problems in the 5.11-5.12 realm. They are all overhanging, though they can be led. The furthest problem on the right side has been led at 5.11.

NINETY-FOOT WALL

This is an excellent crag, seemingly designed for top roping. The climbs cover the full range of difficulties, from 5.1 to 5.12. It is located at the beginning of Eagle Creek Canyon. See the approach and route descriptions in that chapter of this book.

TRIPPY ROCK

Trippy Rock can be found off Highway 27 (Mount Rose Highway) 3.2 miles north of Incline Village. Just before reaching a prominent vista point, turn left onto a dirt road. Drive 200 yards and park. The rock stands 100 yards up and right on the hillside.

BALLBUSTER ROCK

Three miles north of the junction of Highway 50 and Highway 28 at Spooner Summit, this round squat rock sits 50 yards up a hillside to the west. The granite is smooth and solid. The routes are sustained and follow thin faces or well-formed cracks. The longest of the routes is 50 feet, and good natural anchors can be found on top. The difficulty of the 13 established routes ranges from 5.6 to 5.11b.

CRYSTAL BAY BOULDER

This is a 40 foot boulder located midway between King's Beach and Incline Village on the east side of Brockway Hill. To get there, turn off Highway 20 onto Amagosa Street, then turn right on Warsaw Road. Drive to the end of the road and the rock will be visible 50 yards up the hill overlooking Lake Tahoe. The two established crack climbs are 5.9+ and 5.10c.

ICE CLIMBING

Tahoe ice climbing can be very challenging and rewarding when the conditions are right. The climbs are not very long but they offer a variety of difficulties to please both the beginner and the accomplished ice climber. Generally, the approaches are best done on skis but are not very long.

LOVER'S LEAP

It has to be a cold winter to find the rare ice at Lover's Leap, but when it happens, one of the best and most challenging climbs forms here: **Eyeore's Fantasy.** It is 500 feet high and 70 to 90 degrees in steepness.

Ski up the trail that is the normal summer approach, and either ski or slog up the slab to the base. The pitches above Main Ledge form more frequently than the lower section. Once in a while ice also forms in East Gully or in Lover's Chimney. It is advisable to begin these climbs very early in the morning.

MOUNT RALSTON

Mount Ralston's long southeast ridge rises from the southern shore of Echo Lakes. Ice climbing can sometimes be found on the mountain's northeast face in a couloir that rises steeply above the lake. The best approach is from the Echo Lakes Lodge; ski along the south shore of the lake until beneath the face.

LAKE AUDRIAN

At 7300 feet, near the top of Echo Summit, the cliffs above Lake Audrian ices up nearly every winter and provides good ice climbing on faces, slabs and in narrow gullies. Park ½ mile west of Echo Summit in a turn-out on the south side of Highway 50, a few hundred feet above the Little Norway Resort. Ski south across a small bridge and up to a ridge; further south can be seen Lake Audrian and the icy cliffs behind it. Contour the north and east shore of the lake and ski up to the base of the cliffs. The longest lines are about 100 feet, and they can get quite steep. Beware of soft snow on top. To descend, walk west and come down snow slopes.

GUN TOWER CLIFFS

The northeast side of Echo Edge, below Echo Lakes, rises from Highway 50 in a series of slabs and short faces. These frequently ice up in winter and offer short but decent climbs and ice bouldering. On the right side of Highway 50, 1 ½ miles west of the Highway 89 South junction in Meyers, and at the beginnning of the first long left curve in the road, is a brown wooden tower that Caltrans uses to mount the avalanche control howitzer. Park by this platform and follow a snow-covered dirt road to the northwest to the base of small cliffs draped with ice.

It is important to note that the climbs are to the northwest of the highway and not directly above it. Climbing or skiing above the highway is illegal and very unsafe due to the extreme avalanche danger.

ANGORA LAKES

At the northwest end of the Flagpole/Echo Peak crest is the north bowl of Echo Peak. In the bottom of this rocky cirque are the Angora Lakes. A lovely ice climb rises in the cliff band above Upper Angora Lake. Although it has one of the longest approaches of any Tahoe ice climb the general excellence of the route and the ice make the trek worthwhile.

Park at the beginning of the Angora Ridge Road, a dirt road which is closed in the winter. Ski up the road, along the top of the moraine, for two miles to the Angora Lakes Resort, on the northwest shore of Upper Angora Lake. Contour the north and west shore of the lake; the climb is a steep and wide gully about 120 feet high, near the eastern end of the cliff band. To descend, walk north and down to the lake. Be cautious: in times of heavy snow this area is subject to giant avalanches.

CASCADE FALLS

The waterfall at the head of Cascade Lake freezes up nicely in cold times. The ice is low angle but thick. It is a good area for beginners or for ice bouldering. To reach the falls, park off Highway 89 North and start skiing west along the north shore of Cascade Lake. Be careful of private property. At the west end of the lake ski up and right along a streambed in the trees until the wide, frozen falls come into view.

EMERALD BAY AREA

Ice often forms on the small cliffs in Eagle Creek Canyon. Numerous icicles, little slabs and bouldering can be found, mostly on the north facing side of the creek. Up at Eagle Lake, ice climbs form at Eagle Lake Cliffs. One of the better spots is directly across from the creek from Ninety-Foot Wall. Ski up the trail that leads into the Desolation Wilderness, cross the bridge over Eagle Creek, and continue for 100 yards. Cut right off the trail through woods and towards the creek, coming to the base of small, steep slabs. The ice falls range from ten to 40 feet in height.

MAGGIE'S PEAK

Farther up the same trail, on the south side, is Maggie's Peak. Long, steep and thin ice forms in the north facing gullies of this peak, creating technicallly exciting mixed climbing. For details of the approach and descent refer to the Eagle Creek Canyon section of this guide.

Also in the Emerald Bay area, several ice smears can be found on the steep slopes above Highway 89, 200-300 yards south of the bridge over Eagle Falls. **The Inertia Tube** is located 300 yards south of the bridge and 100 feet up the slope. This is a dead vertical, chandeliered icicle that drops from an overhanging bulge. It is often capped by a swelling mushroom of ice. It can be top roped.

CRAG PEAK

This peak is located near the eastern boundary of the Desolation Wilderness, southwest of Rubicon Peak. During cold winters it offers what is perhaps the longest ice climb in the Tahoe region in its north facing gully and chimney system. The ski approach is very long and it is best to plan to camp. There is no easy way to get to this climb but the best seems to be from Eagle Creek Canyon through Rubicon Pass. Refer to the area topographical map to plan your route.

CARSON SPUR

Located on Highway 88 just west of Kirkwood Meadows Ski Resort, this area is not truly in the Tahoe Basin, but deserves special mention due to both its proximity and the often superb ice climbing. From South Lake Tahoe, drive south on Highway 50 to the junction of Highway 89 South. Follow 89 over Luther Pass to the junction of Highway 88. Take 88 west over Carson Pass to the entrance of Kirkwood. For ¾ mile past the Kirkwood area the south side of the Highway is bounded by a terraced cliff that ranges in height from 100 to 500 feet. The rock is a loose volcanic conglomerate, and the ice forms in steep narrow erosion gullies and also in thick icicles and ice curtains that hang from bulges. The climbing is characterized by short steep sections separated by sloping terraces, and during cold spells it becomes possible to link many of these short sections into long and intricate routes.

CAUTION! This area is extremely avalanche-prone. It is unlawful to park or stop your car along this section of the highway, and it is unlawful to walk along the roadside. Park either inside the

Kirkwood entrance road or at the other end of the cliff area in a large plowed turnout on the north side of the highway, and walk or ski along the base of the cliff, away from the road. Exercise good judgement: if the snow seems at all unstable, **DO NOT** approach this area, as you could set loose an avalanche onto the road below.

FIRST ASCENTS

ABUM-DABA var (5.8) Phantom Spires: Kevin Rivett, David Babich, 1978

AERIAL (5.11b tr) Donner: unknown

A FEW DOLLERS MORE (5.10/5.11) Lover's Leap: John Bowlin, John Hoffman, Victor Marcus, Jim Orey, 1977; (direct finish, 5.11): Edwin Drummond

AFTERMATH (5.9) Echo Lakes: Mike Corbett, A. Doehring, 1979

ALIAS EMIL BART (5.10c) Eagle Creek: unknown

A LINE (5.9) Eagle Creek: Rick Sumner, J. Taylor, 1974; (var.) Greg Dexter, Bill Todd, 1976

AL TAHOE (5.9) Lover's Leap: Al Swanson, 1985

ALTAIR (5.10d) Pie Shop: Paul Crawford, John Rosholt, Rick Van Horn, 1977

AMBROSIA (5.7) Pie Shop: unknown

ANCIENT ROUTE (5.7) Pie Shop: unknown

ANT CRACK (5.7) Phantom Spires: unknown

APRIL FOOLS (5.8) Lover's Leap: Gene Drake, Jim Hicks, 1971

AQUALUNG (5.10c) Donner: Gary Allen, Max Jones, 1977

ARCHER (5.8) Pie Shop: unknown

ARROWROOT (5.10c) Lover's Leap: Rick Sumner, Bill Todd, 1975

ATOMIC PUNK (5.10) Eagle Creek: Jay Smith, Paul Crawford, 1982

BABY BEAR (5.10a) Donner: unknown, 1980

BACHAR'S LINE (5.11) Eagle Creek: John Bachar et al

BACK IN BLACK (5.11d) Sugarloaf: Jay Smith, Karl McConachie, 1986

BAD MOON ARISING (5.10c) Lover's Leap: Jay Smith, Foster Green, 1985

BANANA, THE (5.8) Lover's Leap: unknown; FFA: Jim Orey, 1972

BARNEY RUBBLE (5.10a) Eagle Creek: A. Doehring, Mike Corbett, 1980

BASTARD CHILD (5.8) Lover's Leap: Steve Miller, Rick Sumner, 1979

BASTILLE (5.11b tr) Eagle Creek: unknown

BEARHUG (5.9) Lover's Leap: Rick Cashner, Darrel Hatten, 1979

BEAR'S REACH (5.7) Lover's Leap: Phil Berry, Robin Linnett, 1956

BEAST OF BURDEN (5.12) Sugarloaf: Chris Clifford and others, pro placed on rappel, 1984

BEER CAN ALLEY (5.10c) Lover's Leap: Rick Sumner, Bob Pinkney, 1983

BELL BOTTOM BLUES (5.12a) Donner: Kurt Smith, Steve Schneider, 1984

BERTHA BUTT BOOGIE (5.10c) Donner: Max Jones, 1976

BETWEEN THE LINES (5.10a) Lover's Leap: Steve Miller, Rick Sumner, 1981

BIG SLEEP, THE (5.11d) Lover's Leap: Paul Crawford, Karl McConachie, 1986

BLACK MAGIC (5.11c) Lover's Leap: Paul Crawford, Jay Smith, 1980

BLACK OPAL (5.10c) Lover's Leap: N. Booth, Jay Smith, 1979

BLACK PYRE (5.11b) Lover's Leap: Paul Crawford, Jay Smith, 1980

BLACK SEPTEMBER (5.9) Donner: Eric Beck et al, 1973

BLINDFAITH (5.9) Sugarloaf: Jim Orey, John Bowlin, Charley Jones, 1973

BLISS (5.10d) Donner: Max Jones, Victor Marcus, Gary Allen, 1979

BLOCKBUSTER (5.9) Eagle Creek: Mike Corbett, Charlene Serniuk, 1979

BLUE TANGO (A2) Phantom Spires: George Connor, Kevin Rivett, 1978

BLUE WIND (5.10b) Lover's Leap: Jay Smith, Rick Sumner, 1976

BLUFF (5.7) Donner: unknown

BOLEE GOLD (5.10c) Sugarloaf: Garry Anderson, Jay Smith, Rick Sumner, 1977

BOLT RACE (5.11c) Echo Lakes: Paul Crawford Craig Reason, 1986

BOLT RUN (5.10d) Donner: Karl Hammer, John Hoffman, 1974

BOMBS AWAY (5.10b) Lover's Leap: Paul Crawford, Jay Smith, 1980

BOOKIE (5.10) Echo Lakes: Mike Corbett, Charlene Serniuk, 1980

BOOKMARK (5.7) Lover's Leap: Steve Thompson, Gordon Webster, 1966; above Main Ledge: P. Berry, R. Linnett, 1954

BOOTHILL (5.11a) Lover's Leap: Paul Crawford, Paul Obanheim, Jay Smith, 1984

BOPPY'S CRACK (5.8) Echo Lakes: Mike Corbett, Bill Serniuk, 1979

BOTTOMLESS TOPLESS (5.10a) Donner: unknown

BOURBON STREET (5.10a) Donner: Gary Allen, John Hoffman, Malcolm Jolly, 1977

BRAIN CHILD (5.12 tr) Donner: Christian Griffith, 1980

BREAK OUT (5.8) Donner: unknown

BRIDWELL'S CLIMB (5.11a tr) Donner: Jim Bridwell, 1976

B.T. EXPRESS (5.9) Pie Shop: Rick Sumner, Bill Todd, 1974

BURNT OFFERINGS (5.10d) Phantom Spires: Paul Crawford, Don Garret, 1982

BURNT PIE (5.3) Pie Shop: unknown

BURROWING OWL (5.7) Phantom Spires: Kevin Rivett, 1974

BUSHFREAK CORNER (5.8) Echo Lakes: unknown

BUSHFREAK ELIMINATE (5.8) Echo Lakes; unknown

BUSTER BROWN (5.10b) Eagle Creek: Rick Cashner, Mike Corbett, 1979

BUZZARD, THE (5.11b) Eagle Creek: Jay Smith, Paul Crawford, P. Obanheim, 1985

BYPASS (5.10d) Donner: Max Jones et al, 1979

CANDYLAND (5.10c) Phantom Spires: Eric Barrett, John Bowlin, Robert Oravetz, 1977

CANNIBAL GULLY (5.7) Donner: Bill Dutton, Paul Sullivan, 1969

CAPTAIN COCONUTS (5.10a) Lover's Leap: Paul Crawford, Richard Harrison, Nick Nordblum, 1982

CAPTAIN FINGERS (5.12c) Sugarloaf: Gene Drake, Jim Hicks, 1970; FFA: Mark Hudon, Max Jones, 1979

CARLY ANN'S BUTTERFLIES (5.8) Lover's Leap: Michael Stevenson, Don Seawell, 1984

CASUAL OBSERVER (5.1) Eagle Creek: unknown

CENTRAL GULLY (5.6) Donner: unknown

CHAINSAW WILLIE (5.8) Phantom Spires: David Babich, 1982

CHANGELING (5.8) Eagle Creek: Paul Tear, K. Haddock, 1982

CHANGE UP (5.8) Donner: Gene Drake, Jim Silfrast, 1977

CHAR- BROILED (5.10d) Phantom Spires: Karl McConachie, Paul Crawford, 1984

CHEAP SHOT (5.10a) Lover's Leap: Jay Smith, Paul Crawford, 1982

CLEAN CORNER (5.8) Pie Shop: Steve Miller, Jay Smith, 1980

CLONEDIKE, THE (5.9) Lover's Leap: Rick Sumner, Jeff Altenberg, Maggie ALtenberg, 1981

CLOWN, THE (5.8) Phantom Spires: Kevin Rivett, David Croy, Robert Oravetz, 1979

COCKABOOTY (5.7) Phantom Spires: unknown

COMPOSURE (5.6) Donner: unknown

COQUETT (5.8) Phantom Spires: Kevin Rivett, David Babich, 1978

CORKSCREW (5.7) Echo Lakes: unknown

CORNFLAKES (5.9) Phantom Spires: Robert Oravetz, Eric Barrett, Dave Starn, 1978

CORRUGATION CORNER (5.7) Lover's Leap: K. Edsburg et al, early 1960's

CRACK OF THE EIGHTIES (5.12) Donner: Alan Watts, 1985

CRACKULA (5.10a) Eagle Creek: Rick Cashner and Bill Serniuk, 1979

CRASH LANDING (5.10a) Lover's Leap: Karl McConachie, Jay Smith, Randy Grandstaff, 1982

CRAVEN IMAGE (5.7) Lover's Leap: Royal Robbins, Steve Roper, 1969

CRAWDADDYS IN FLIGHT (5.10c) Lover's Leap: Paul Crawford, Eric Alexander, 1982

CRAZY DAZE (5.9) Lover's Leap: Jay Smith, Rick Sumner, 1978

CRAZY LACE (5.9) Lover's Leap: Jeff Altenburg, Grant Altenburg, Jerre Akers, Chuck Clance, 1975

CREAM PUFF (5.7) Pie Shop: unknown

CREAM PUFF (5.10b) Donner: John Hoffman, 1983

CREPES CORNER (5.7) Pie Shop: unknown

CRISPY CRITTERS (5.10a) Phantom Spires: Bill Price, Paul Crawford, Jay Smith, 1981

CRITERION, THE (5.11a) Eagle Creek: Jay Smith, Paul Obanheim, J. Mitchel, 1981

CROSS TOWN TRAFFIC, THE (5.11a) Lover's Leap: Karl McConachie, Paul Crawford, Jay Smith, 1981

CRUISE CONTROL (5.8) Pie Shop: D. Nidever, Kevin Nelson, 1981

CRUD GULLY (5.8) Lover's Leap: Royal Robbins, Steve Roper, 1969

CRY MARY (A3) Sugerloaf: Bill Todd, 1977; FFA: (5.12 tr) Jay Smith, 1984

CRYSTALLINE DREAM (5.9) Echo Lakes: unknown

CUCUMBER SLUMBER (5.10b) Donner: Gary Allen, Max Jones

DANCIN' FEET (5.10d) Jeff and Maggie Altenburg, Jay Smith, 1980

DAVE'S RUN (5.11b tr) Eagle Creek: unknown

DAYDREAMS (5.9 A1; 5.10 var.) Phantom Spires: Eric Barrett, George Connor, 1976

DEAD TREE DIRECT (5.7) Lover's Leap: Bob Grow, John Harwood, 1971

DEATH TUNA (5.10) Echo Lakes: Don Garret, Rick Van Horn, Paul Crawford, 1983

DECEPTION (5.6) Lover's Leap: Gene Drake, Larry Morris, 1969

DELUSION OF DESPERATION (5.10a) Donner: unknown

DEVALUATION (5.7) Donner: unknown

DELIVERANCE (5.9+) Pie Shop: unknown

DER FÜRHER (5.11d) Eagle Creek: Jay Smith, Paul Crawford, P. Obanheim, 1985

DESIDERATA (5.10b) Pie Shop: Bill Todd, 1976

DESPERADO ROOF VAR. (5.10b) Phantom Spires: David Babich, George Connor, 1978

DEVIATE (5.8) Lover's Leap: Ben Borson, Tom Higgins, 1968

DIAGONAL (5.9) Sugarloaf: unknown

DIRTY DOG (5.10c) Sugarloaf: unknown

DIRTY HARRY (5.9) Lover's Leap: Kevin Nelson, D. Nedever, 1981

DIRECT (5.8) Lover's Leap: unknown

DR. JECKEL AND MR. HIDE (5.11a) Phantom Spires: Tom Smith, Krista Smith, Larry Von Wald, 1984

DONNER DELIGHT (5.8) Donner: Gary Allen, 1977

DOMINION (5.10a) Sugarloaf: Gene Drake, Dan Hart, Jim Orey, 1972

DROPOUT (5.10d) Pie Shop: unknown; FFA: Richard Harrison, Jay Smith, 1977

DROPOUTS, THE (5.10b-5.11b) Donner: (left) Max Jones, 1977; (right) Karl Hammer, 1976; (far right) Louise Sheppard, 1981

DRUG CRAZED (5.11c) Lover's Leap: Tony Yaniro, Max Jones, 1984

DUMBO (5.9) Echo Lakes: Paul Crawford, free solo, 1986

EAGLE BUTTRESS LEFT SIDE (5.8) Lover's Leap: P. Berry, R. Linnett, 1956

EAGLE BUTTRESS RIGHT SIDE (5.9) Lover's Leap: TM Herbert, Gordon Webster, 1966

EAGLE'S HIGHWAY (5.8) Lover's Leap: Brian Chandler, Steve Miller, 1978

EAGLE ROUTE (5.5) Eagle Creek: Dave Beck, Norm Wilson, 1963

EARN YOUR WINGS (5.9) Pie Shop: B. Crawford, C. Crawford, 1979

EASIER SAID THAN DONE (5.10d) Lover's Leap: Richard Harrison Jay Smith, 1981

EASIER THAN IT LOOKS (5.7) Lover's Leap: M. Gurrish, Bob Pinkney, P. McCouglha, 1980

EAST CHIMNEY (5.7) Sugarloaf: unknown

EAST ARETE (5.10b) Phantom Spires: David Babich, Don Spitter, 1977; FFA: Jay Smith, Jo Bentley, Karl McConachie, 1986

EAST CORNER (5.10d) Lover's Leap: TM Herbert, Bob Kamps, 1969

EAST CORNER (5.9) Sugarloaf: Gene Drake, Jim Hicks, 1969

EAST CRACK (5.8) Lover's Leap: TM Herbert, Gordon Webster, 1966

EAST FACE (5.9) Phantom Spires: George Connor, D. Chan, 1976

EAST FACE LIZARD HEAD (5.10c tr) Phantom Spires: Jay Smith, 1986

EAST OF EYORE (5.7) Lover's Leap: P. Berry, R. Linnett, 1954

EAST RIDGE ROUTE (5.7) Eagle Creek: Rick Sumner, Bill Todd, solo, 1974

EAST WALL (5.6) Lover's Leap: Ken Edsburg, Mike Edsburg, J. Sublette, 1964

E.B.'s WALL (5.10b) Echo Lakes: Kevin Nelson, Bill Todd, 1974

ELECTRA (5.9 A2) Phantom Spires: Kevin Rivett, David Babich, 1977

ELEVENTH GRADE CORNER (5.8) Donner: unknown

EMPTY OVERGO (5.10a) Donner: unknown

EMPTY SKY (5.10a) Donner: Max Jones, Geoff Smith, 1977

END OF THE LINE (5.10b) Lover's Leap: Jay Smith, Karl Mc-Conachie, Paul Crawford, 1984

EPITAPH (5.10c) Lover's Leap: Paul Obanheim, Brian Harrington, Chris Bay, 1985

ERASER HEAD (5.10b) Phantom Spires: David Babich, Kevin Rivett, 1980

EYES OF SILVER (5.10c) Donner: Dick Richardson, Malcolm Jolly, 1977

EXCELSIOR (5.10a) Lover's Leap: Richard Harrison, Jay Smith, 1977

EYORE'S ECSTACY (5.7) Lover's Leap: P. Berry, R. Linnett, 1957 above Main Ledge: Frank DeSaussure et al, 1953; FFA: Al McDonald, Steve Roper, 1959

EYORE'S ENIGMA (5.9+) Lover's Leap: Warren Harding, TM Herbert, Galen Rowell, 1969; FFA: Jim Orey et al, 1973

FALLOUT (5.9 tr) Eagle Creek: unknown

FANDANGO (5.9−) Lover's Leap: George Connor, David Babich, 1978

FANCY DANCIN' (5.10) Phantom Spires: Robert Oravetz, Eric Barrett, 1978

FANG left side, THE (5.9) Sugarloaf: Jim Orey, M. Vincent, 1971

FANTASIA (5.9) Lover's Leap: Royal Robbins, Ken Wilson, 1973

FARCE, THE (5.4) Lover's Leap: unknown

FAR EAST (5.9) Lover's Leap: Jay Smith, Paul Obanheim, 1980

FAREWELL TO ARMS (5.10b) Donner Summit: Karl Hammer, John Hoffman, 1976

FARLEY (5.9) Sugarloaf: Eric Beck, Steve Roper, mid 1960's; knobby wall finish: Jim Orey, 1971

FASCINATION (5.10c) Donner: Gary Allen, Max Jones, 1977

FAT MERCHANTS CRACK (5.10a) Sugarloaf: Royal Robbins et al, 1967

FEAR NO EVIL (5.9) Lover's Leap: Norm Booth, Jay Smith, 1979

FEAR OF FLYING (5.9) Phantom Spires: Bob Grow, J. Moore, 1975; FFA: Eric Barrett, George Connor, 1977; 5.10b var: Mark Hudon, Gary Anderson, 1980

FEAR OF FLYING (5.9) Pie Shop: B. Crawford, P. Crawford, 1978

FINGER GRAFFITTI (5.11c tr) Donner: aided in the 60's

FINGERLICKER (5.10d) Donner: (1st pitch) Ron Kauk, 1975; (2nd pitch) Max Jones, Gary Allen, 1977

FINGERLOCK (5.10b) Sugarloaf: Jim Orey, 1972

FIRECRACKER (5.10b) Donner: Jim Bridwell, 1976

FIREWORKS (5.9) Lover's Leap: Greg Dexter, Steve Miller, 1976

FLAKY FLAKES (5.10b) Lover's Leap: Earl Redfern, Mike Rede

FLAT HEAD (5.9) Phantom Spires: Eric Barrett, David Babich, 1978

FLIGHT DECK (5.11d) Sugarloaf: Blair Haffly, Paul Brown, 1985

FLUTED CRUST (5.5) Pie Shop: unknown

FLYING CIRCUS (5.10a) Lover's Leap: Steve Miller, Jay Smith, Karl Jenkewitz, 1982

FLYING HIGH (5.10a) Lover's Leap: R. Bobzien, Jay Smith, Tim Washick, 1980

FLYTRAP (5.7) Sugarloaf: unknown

FOR REAL CRACK (5.8) Lover's Leap: Gene Drake, M. Haymond, Jim Hicks, 1971

FULL MOON (5.11d) Donner: Max Jones, Gary Allen, 1978

FULL TILT (5.11a) Donner: Dale Bard, 1977

FUSE, THE (5.10c) Donner: Max Jones, Gary Allen, 1978

FUTURE GAMES (5.10b) Donner: unknown

GALLOWS POLE (5.11b) Sugarloaf: Paul Crawford, Rick Van Horn, 1982

GAMOKE, THE (5.8) Lover's Leap: Richard Harrison, Jay Smith, 1977

GHOST IN THE MACHINE, THE (5.12a) Sugarloaf: Ed Drummond, Mark Robinson, 1984

GINGERBREAD (5.7) Phantom Spires: George Connor, Robert Oravetz, 1975

GIVE ME SLACK (5.7) Donner: Gene Drake 1980

GLAZE-HER-FACE (5.11a A1) Lover's Leap: Paul Crawford, Jay Smith, Rick Van Horn, 1980

GOD OF THUNDER (5.11c/d) Lover's Leap: Dario Gambetta, Tony Yaniro, 1978

GOLD DUST (5.10d) Donner: Max Jones, 1977

GOLDILOCKS (5.10d) Donner: unknown

GOLDEN YEARS (5.11a) Echo Lakes: Paul Crawford, Paul Tears, Fletcher Wilson, 1984

GOLD METTLE (5.11d/5.12a) Eagle Creek: Paul Crawford, 1983

GO MAN, THE (5.9) Phantom Spires: Kevin Rivett, David Babich, 1978

GRAND DELUSION (5.12) Sugarloaf: unknown; FFA: Chris Clifford

GRAND ILLUSION (5.13c) Sugarloaf: unknown; FFA: Tony Yaniro, 1979

GREASE (5.12) Donner: Rob Settlemire, 1981

GREEN HORNET (5.11c tr) Donner: unknown

GRIN AND BARE IT (5.10a) Echo Lakes: Bill Todd, 1976

GROOVE, THE (5.7) Lover's Leap: Rockcraft instructors, 1970

HAIR PIE (5.9) Pie Shop: unknown

HAIR SHIRT (5.8) Donner: unknown

HAM AND EGGS (5.9 A1) Phantom Spires: David Croy, Robert Oravetz, 1977

HAM SANDWICH (5.9) Lover's Leap: unknown

HANDS MASSEUSE (5.8) Pie Shop: Paul Crawford, Mike Shreve, 1976

HANGING JUGS (5.8) Sugarloaf: Gene Drake, M. Haymond, 1969

HARDING'S CHIMNEY (5.7) Sugarloaf: Warren Harding, John Ohrenschall, 1954

HARDING'S OTHER CHIMNEY (5.6) Phantom Spires: Warren Harding, John Ohrenschall, 1954

HARD RIGHT (5.10c) Sugarloaf: Karl McConachie, Al Swanson, 1986

HARD-UP var. (5.10) Phantom Spires: Eric Barrett, D. Stam, 1977

HARVEY'S WALLBANGERS (5.6-5.8) Lover's Leap: unknown

HAYSTACK CRACK (5.8) Lover's Leap: Ken Edsburg, TM Herbert, Jerry Sublette, 1965

HEAD EAST (5.9) Pie Shop: unknown

HEADJAMMER (5.8) Pie Shop: Greg Dexter, Steve Miller, 1976

HEADSTONE (5.11b) Donner: Mark Hudon, 1977

HEMORRHOIDS IN FLIGHT (5.10c) Lover's Leap: Rick Cashner, Darrell Hatten, Rick Sumner, 1979

HERMIT, THE (5.9) Pie Shop: Bill Todd, Rick Sumner, 1974

HIGH TOUR (5.9) Lover's Leap: Greg Dexter, Steve Miller, Jay Smith, 1977

HINDSIGHT (5.8) Pie Shop: unknown

HIT AND RUN (5.7) Echo Lakes: Rick Cashner, Mike Corbett, Bill Serniuk, 1979

HOLDLESS HORROR (5.6) Eagle Creek: unknown

HOOK, THE (5.11d) Donner: unknown

HOOKER'S HAVEN (5.12a) Sugarloaf: Jim Orey, Charlie Jones, 1971; FFA: Mark Hudon, Max Jones, 1978

HORNBLOWER (5.8) Greg Dexter, Steve Miller, 1976

HOSPITAL CORNER (5.10a) Lover's Leap: unknown; FFA: Richard Harrison, Jay Smith, 1977

HOT SHIT (5.10b) Donner: John Hoffman, 1977

HOURGLASS, THE (5.11a) Lover's Leap: Warren Harding, Dick Long, Jack Rankin, 1965; FFA: Greg Dexter, Rick Sumner, 1975

HOURGLASS WALL (5.11c) Lover's Leap: Jeff Lowe, 1969; FFA: Paul Crawford, Bill Price, 1982

HUMBLE PIE (5.7) Pie Shop: unknown

HUNGOVER-HANGOVER (5.10a) Donner: Craig Shanholtzer, Dick Dorworth, 1975

HYPERSPACE (5.10b) Sugarloaf: Richard Harrison, Jay Smith, 1977

ICE NINE (5.10a tr) Eagle Creek: unknown

IF I HAD A HAMMER (5.11b) Al Swanson, Fred Cohen, Charlene Serniuk, 1985

IMAGINARY VOYAGE (5.11c) Donner: Max Jones, Gary Allen, 1977

INCUBUS (5.10b) Lover's Leap: Royal Robbins, Steve Roper, 1972

INSIDE OUT (5.8) Donner: (lower section) Eric Beck, Harry Smeenk, A.P.Marsten, 1970; (upper section) Barry Dow, Dan Schultz, 1970

INSIDIOUS (5.6) Donner: John Hoffman, free solo, 1972

I'M GUNBY DUMMIT (5.9) Eagle Creek: Morgan Kent, Dvorack

JACK CORNER (5.9) Phantom Spires: David Babich, D. Spittler, 1976; FFA: Eric Barrett, Dave Stam, 1976

JACK CRACK, THE (5.10d) Eagle Creek: Paul Crawford, solo, 1986

JACK OF HEARTS (5.10a) Donner: Gary Allen, Max Jones, 1977

JAILBREAK (5.8) Lover's Leap: T. Kesler, Rick Sumner, 1976·

JAM SESSION (5.10a) Echo Lakes: unknown

JAM SESSION (5.10b) Donner: unknown

JEFF'S FOLLY (5.7) Lover's Leap: M. Caldwell, R. Erdman, J. Fowler, C. Williams, 1969

JELLYROLL ARCH (5.8) Donner: John Hoffman, Skip Casey, 1972

JOE YOUNG (5.8 A2) Phantom Spires: Eric Barrett, David Babich, 1977

JUGS REVISITED (5.9) Phantom Spires: George Connor, Robert Oravetz, 1975

JULY (5.8) Phantom Spires: Kevin Rivett, David Babich, 1976

JUNIOR HIGH (5.6) Donner: unknown

J. WALK (5.7) Pie Shop: Tom Condon, R. Jamieson, 1971

KANGAROO (5.10b) Echo Lakes: John Bowlin, Jim Day, Jim Orey, 1979

KARL'S GYM (5.10d) Donner: Karl Hammer, 1974

KARL'S OVERHANG (5.11a) Donner: Karl Hammer, solo, 1975

K.E. CRACKS (5.11) Phantom Spires: George Connor, Robert Oravetz, 1976; FFA: Eric Barrett, David Stam, 1981

KINDERGARTEN (5.6) Donner: unknown

KNAPSACK CRACK (5.3) Lover's Leap: unknown

KNEE-ON (5.10b) Echo Lakes: Rick Cashner, Mike Corbett, 1979

KNOBHILL (5.7) Pie Shop: unknown

KNOBJOB (5.6) Pie Shop: Steve Miller, Jay Smith, 1977

KO-KO BOX (5.7) Phantom Spires: Kevin Rivett, David Babich, 1974

LABYRINTH (5.6) Donner: John Hoffman, Bob Carter, Paul Schimmon, Ken Volz, 1972

LA CHUTE (5.10a) Phantom Spires: George Connor, Kevin Rivett, 1979

LADY LUCK (5.10a) Sugarloaf: Luke Freeman, Bill Todd, 1976

LASER TREATMENT (5.11b) Donner: Gene Drake, Mark Robinson, 1979

LAST DANCE, THE (5.11b) Pie Shop: Rick Van Horn, 1980

LAST LAUGH (5.10a) Lover's Leap: Richard Harrison, Jay Smith, 1977

LAST SANDWICH, THE (5.9) Lover's Leap: Steve Miller, Will Cottrell, 1984

LAST TANGO (5.11c) Donner: Mark Hudon, 1979

LEAN AND MEAN (5.9) Phantom Spires: Bob Grow, J. Moore, 1976

LEAPIN' LIZARDS (5.9) Echo Lakes: Mike Corbett, Charlene Serniuk, 1979

LIL' LUKE (5.9) Phantom Spires: Kevin Rivett, David Babich, 1978; FFA: Eric Barrett, John Bowlin, 1980

LIGHTNING BOLT (5.10b tr) Eagle Creek: unknown

LIGHTNING BOLT ROOF (5.11a) Donner: Jim Orey, 1977

LINE, THE (5.9) Lover's Leap: TM Herbert, Doug Tompkins, 1966; FFA: Tom Higgins, Frank Sarnquist, 1968

LITTLE FEAT (5.10d) Donner: Max Jones, Gary Allen, 1979

LITTLE SIR ECHO (5.11 + tr) Echo Lakes: Paul Crawford, 1984

LOST AND FOUND (5.9) Eagle Creek: Mike Corbett, Bill Serniuk

LOST IN SPACE (5.11a tr) Eagle Creek: unknown

LOST IN THE FOG (5.9 A2) Sugarloaf: Bill Todd, 1977

LOVER'S CHIMNEY (5.5) Lover's Leap: Bruce Cooke, 1949

LURCH (5.8) Sugarloaf: Jim Hicks, Larry Morris, 1971

MAD DOG (5.10c) Sugarloaf: unknown

MAD WIFE (5.8) Pie Shop: D. Nidever, K. Nelson, 1981

MAGNUM FORCE (5.10c) Lover's Leap: Greg Dexter, Jay Smith, 1977

MAINLINE (5.11c) Lover's Leap: Jay Smith, Bill Todd, 1976; FFA: John Bachar, Ron Kauk, 1978

MAGIC BOOK (5.8) Echo Lakes: Mike Corbett, Bill Serniuk, Charlene Serniuk, 1979

MAKE THAT MOVE RIGHT NOW BABY (5.10c) Sugarloaf: M. Stumpf, B. Albonico, 1981

MAMA BEAR (5.11a) Donner: Gary Allen, 1977

MAN WHO FELL TO EARTH, THE (5.11b) Sugarloaf: Mark Hudon, Max Jones, 1979

MANGOD (5.11a) Echo Lakes: Vaino Kodas, Al Swanson, 1985

MANIC DEPRESSION (5.11c) Donner: Max Jones, 1976

MANIC DEPRESSIVE (5.8) Lover's Leap: Bill Chandler, S. Garofalos, Kevin Nelson, 1980

MANNY, THE (5.12 tr) Eagle Creek: Paul Crawford, 1986

MARY'S CRACK (5.8) Donner

MARMOT PIE (5.8 A4) Pie Shop: Cactus Joe Bryan, Jeff Lowe, 1971

MASTER OF DISASTER (5.10a) Eagle Creek: Paul Obanheim, J. Mitchell, 1985

MASTER RACE (5.11c) Eagle Creek: Jay Smith, Paul Crawford, Paul Obanheim, 1985

M.D.A. (5.9) Lover's Leap: Jay Smith, Rick Sumner, 1976

MEAN MOE (5.10c) Phantom Spires: Robert Oravetz, George Connor, 1979

MIDDLE AGES (5.8) Donner: Gene Drake, Jim Silfrast, 1979

MILLER'S HIGHLIFE (5.9) Pie Shop: Steve Miller, solo, 1976

MINCEMEAT VARIATION (5.9) Pie Shop: unknown

MINOTAUR (5.7) Donner: John Hoffman, Fred Andregg, 1972

MR. CLEAN (5.10c/d) Donner: Victor Marcus, Malcolm Jolly, Jim Day, 1977

MISSING MIND (5.11c tr) Donner: unknown

MITIGATE (5.7) Donner: Ken Volz, Ron Clegg

MO CRACK, THE (5.10a) Eagle Creek: Paul Crawford, 1986

MOLAR CONCENTRATION (5.10b) Donner: John Hoffman, Victor Marcus, 1977

MOLE'S CORNER (5.8) Donner: Tom Garamic, Gary Allen, Max Jones, 1976

MONKEY BUSINESS (5.10a) Eagle Creek: Rick Sumner, Bill Todd, 1974

MONKEY PAWS (5.12a) Donner: Max Jones, 1979

MOONRAKER (5.10a) Donner: Rick Cashner, Angie Morales, 1979

MOONSHINE (5.9) Donner: unknown

MORE MADNESS (5.11b) Lover's Leap: Karl McConachie, Paul Crawford, 1984

MOSS PIE (5.8) Pie Shop: Bill Crawford, D. Dvorak, 1972

MOUNTAINEER'S ROUTE (class 4) Eagle Creek: unknown

NAGUAL, THE (5.10c) Eagle Creek: Bill Todd, 1976; FFA: Rick Cashner, Angie Morales, 1979

NATURAL HIGH (5.11c) Pie Shop: D. Waters, 1973; FFA: Paul Crawford, Rick Van Horn, 1980

NECKLACE TRAVERSE (5.10d) Phantom Spires: George Connor, D. Chan, 1977; FFA: George Connor, Robert Oravetz, 1979

NEVER ENDING STORY (5.11 tr) Eagle Creek: unknown

NEW FASCINATON (5.10d) Donner: unknown

NEW MOON (5.10d) Donner: John Hoffman, Max Jones, 1976

NEXT (5.10d) Donner: (2nd pitch) Eric Beck, 1972; (3rd pitch) Max Jones, Gary Allen, 1977

NIGHT COUNTRY (5.11b) Donner: John Hoffman, Victor Marcus, 1979

NIGHT GALLERY (5.10b) Donner: Eric Pedman, Dick Dorworth

NO FUTURE (5.9) Pie Shop: S. Bushy, Paul Crawford, Eric Alexander, 1977

NORTH COUNTRY (5.10a) Lover's Leap: Charley Jones, Victor Marcus, Jim Orey, C. Stanborough, 1975

NORTH DIAGONAL (5.9) Lover's Leap: Ken Edsburg and friends, mid-60's

NORTH FACE Lizard Head (5.11c tr) Phantom Spires: Jay Smith, 1986

NORTH FACE (5.11a) Lover's Leap: K. Edsburg, J. Davidson, 1963 (aid pitch free) M. Andrews, Jim Orey; (first pitch var.) Paul Crawford, 1979

NO STEMS NO SEEDS (5.10d) Donner: Max Jones, Gary Allen, 1977

NOVA EXPRESS (5.9) Donner: unknown

NOVITIATE'S NIGHTMARE (5.9) Lover's Leap: unknown

NUMBER, THE (5.7) Lover's Leap: D. Ketchum, K. Ranen, 1971

OEDIPUS REX (5.7) Phantom Spires: Kevin Rivett, David Babich, 1975

OFF THE WALL (5.10b) Eagle Creek: D. Rennick, K. Volz, 1973; FFA unknown

OFFWIDTH THEIR HEADS (5.9) Echo Lakes: Rick Cashner, Mike Corbett, 1979

OKTOBER FEST (5.10c) Phantom Spires: Paul Brown, David Babich, 1985

OLD PECULIAR (5.8) Echo Lakes: Mike Corbett, Bill Serniuk, Charlene Serniuk, 1979

ONE HAND CLAPPING (5.9) Donner: (1st pitch) Kim Schmitz, A.P. Marsten, 1972; (2nd pitch) Eric Beck, Peter Haan, 1972

101 DALMATIONS (5.10c) Phantom Spires: Tom Smith, Krista Smith, Larry Von Wald, 1984

ONE MORE FOR THE ROAD (5.10d tr) Eagle Creek: unknown

ON RAMP (5.8) Donner: Kim Schmitz, Norm Simmons, 1971

ORANGE BOOK (5.8) Eagle Creek: P. Arthur, Dick Dorworth, 1970

ORANGE SUNSHINE (5.9) Eagle Creek: K. Nelson, Bill Todd, 1974

OUT TO LUNGE (5.10d) Lover's Leap: Steve Miller, 1978

OVER EASY (5.7) Phantom Spires: George Connor, Robert Oravetz

OVER THE TOP (5.11a) Donner: unknown

OZZIE (5.10a) Lover's Leap: Paul Crawford, Richard Harrison, Nick Nordblum, 1982

PALSY (5.9) Donner: unknown

PANIC IN DETROIT (5.12c) Donner: Max Jones, 1979

PAPA BEAR (5.10a) Donner: Max Jones, 1976

PARAMOUR (5.9) Lover's Leap: Eric Bjornstad, B. Hagen, 1968; FFA: Greg Dexter, Rick Sumner, 1975

PEA SOUP (5.9) Donner: unknown

PEANUT BRITTLE (5.7) Lover's Leap: Gene Drake, H. Haymond, 1969

PEBBLE IN THE SKY (5.10a) Donner: John Hoffman, Victor Marcus, 1984

PETER PRINCIPLE (5.10a) Donner: Karl Hammer, 1975

PIE FACE DIHEDRAL (5.9) Pie Shop: Steve Miller, Jay Smith, 1978

PIE IN THE SKY (5.7) Pie Shop: Cactus Bryan, Paul Crawford, 1971

PIECE OF MIND (5.10c) Lover's Leap: Edwin Drummond, Lanny Johnson, 1981

PIGS ON THE WING (5.10a) Lover's Leap: Jay Smith, Rick Sumner, 1977

PILLAR OF SOCIETY (5.11) Lover's Leap: Chris Clifford, Chris Pitman, 1984

PINBALL JUNKIE (5.11a) Donner: unknown

PIPS PILAR (5.8) Lover's Leap: Kevin Nelson, B. Chandler, S. Garf, 1980

PITCHFORK (5.8-5.10a) Echo Lakes: unknown

PLATITUDE (5.8) Phantom Spires: David Coy, David Babich, Joe Metz, 1985

POLAR CIRCUS (5.11c tr) Eagle Creek: unknown

POLECAT (A3) Eagle Creek: Bill Todd, 1976

POLY GRIP (5.10c) Pie Shop: Paul Crawford, Rick Van Horn, 1980

PONY EXPRESS (5.9) Sugarloaf: (1st pitch) Dick Long, mid-60's; (2nd pitch) Gene Drake, Jim Hicks, 1970

POP BOTTLE (5.6) Lover's Leap: Gene Drake, M. Haymond, Larry Morris, 1969

PORNO BOOK (5.8) Donner: unknown

PREPARATION H (5.8) Lover's Leap: M. Haymond, Jim Hicks, 1969

PRIMER (5.9) Donner: unknown

PRICE IS LIGHT, THE (5.10c tr) Pie Shop: Alan Swanson, Bill Price, 1985

PSYCHEDELIC TREE (5.9) Lover's Leap: Bruce Cooke, TM Herbert, 1968

PRICE-SMITH ROUTE (5.10d) Phantom Spires: Bill Price, Jay Smith, 1983

PROTECTION DIFFICULT (5.8) Donner: Gary Allen, 1977

PURPLE HAZE (5.10d) Lover's Leap: Richard Harrison, Jay Smith, 1977

PYRAMID (5.10) Echo Lakes: Paul Crawford, Paul Obanheim, 1983

QUEST FOR GLORY (5.10d) Eagle Creek: D. Frixbee and friends, 1983

RAMP, THE (5.8) Echo Lakes: J. Bowlin, D. Johnson, J. Leonard, Jim Orey, A. Price, 1979

RAPID TRANSIT (5.8) Donner: unknown

RAIN SONG (5.7) Phantom Spires: David Babich, 1980

RASBERRY BYPASS (5.10b) Lover's Leap: D. Knight

RATED X (5.8-5.9) Lover's Leap: Eric Beck, Peter Haan, 1972

RATED X DIRECT (5.11b) Lover's Leap: Jim Orey, F. Van Overbeck, 1972; FFA: Kark McConachie, Jay Smith, 1984

RAT'S TOOTH (5.10a) Donner: unknown

REDNECKS (5.9) Lover's Leap: Rick Sumner, Bill Todd, 1976

REDS DELIGHT (5.9) Lover's Leap: Red and friends

REGULAR ROUTE Lower Spire (5.9) Phantom Spires: R. Moreau, R. Hoopes, 1955

REGULAR ROUTE Middle Spire (5.8) Phantom Spires: unknown

REGULAR ROUTE Upper Spire (5.5) Phantom Spires: unknown

REHUMANIZE YOURSELF (A3) Echo Lakes: John Akens, Jay Smith, Karl Jenkewitz, 1982

RELATIVITY (5.10b tr) Eagle Creek: unknown

RENTIER (5.7 tr) Eagle Creek: unknown

RIPOFF (5.10 tr) Eagle Creek: unknown

ROBERT'S CRACK (5.10c) Phantom Spires: George Connor, Robert Oravetz, 1975; FFA: Eric Barrett, John Bowlin, 1979

ROCKY (5.5) Donner: unknown

ROOFER MADNESS (5.10c) Lover's Leap: Jay Smith, Rick Sumner, 1977

ROUGH AND READY (5.8) Echo Lakes: unknown

ROCK-A-BYE-BABY (5.9) Echo Lakes: Al Swanson, Charlene Serniuk, 1985

SANITATION CRACK (5.10c) Donner: Max Jones, 1977

SAW, THE (5.5) Pie Shop: Bill Crawford, M. Franceschini, Dan Dvorak, Rick Jamieson 1973

SAYONARA (5.7) Echo Lakes: Mike Corbett, Bill Serniuk, Charlene Serniuk, 1979

SCHEISTER (5.7) Sugarloaf: unknown, probably in the 1950's

SCIMITAR (5.9) Lover's Leap: Mike Covington, Dick Erb, 1969; FFA: Jim Orey, F. Van Overbeck, 1972

SCORPIO (5.7) Sugarloaf: Jay Smith, Rick Sumner, J. Taylor, 1977

SCRATCHIN' NAILS (5.10b) Donner: Max Jones, solo, 1979

SEAMS TO ME (5.10c) Eagle Creek: D. Grossman, R. Van Horn, 1980

SECTION 20 (5.7) Eagle Creek: (lower section) Doug Tompkins, 1963; (upper section) P. Arthur, 1967

SEEMS TO ME (5.11d tr) Donner: unknown

SELF ABUSE (5.10b) Phantom Spires: Royal Robbins, 1967

SENIOR PROM (5.9) Donner: unknown

SEPARATED REALITY (5.8) Eagle Creek: R. Clegg, K Volz, 1973

SETTLE DOWN (5.9) Lover's Leap: unknown

SEVEN-ELEVEN CRACKS (5.8-5.10c) Pie Shop: Alan Swanson, Ken Black, Mark Bauer, 1985

SHADY LADY (5.8) Lover's Leap: Jim Hicks, Ralph Regua, 1970

SHELOB'S LAIR (5.9) Pie Shop: Bill Todd, 1976

SHOOT OUT (5.8) Donner: unknown

SHORT CAKE (5.6) Pie Shop: Steve Miller, Jay Smith, 1978

SHORT CAKE (5.9) Donner: John Hoffman, 1983

SHORTS ONLY (5.9) Lover's Leap: Kevin Nelson, B. Chandler, 1980

SHUMAN THE HUMAN (5.7 tr) Eagle Creek: unknown

SICKLE, THE (5.8) Lover's Leap: Gene Drake, Jim Hicks, 1970

SIDE EFFECT (5.9) Donner: John Hoffman, Victor Marcus, 1977

SILLY WILLY CRACK, THE (5.12c) Lover's Leap: Bill Price, 1982

SILVER BOOK (5.7) Donner: Max Jones, 1976

SIMPLE SIMON (5.2) Pie Shop: unknown

SINGE CITY (5.11b) Phantom Spires: Jay Smith, Karl McConachie, 1986

SIZZLER (5.11b) Phantom Spires: Jay Smith, Paul Crawford, 1986; Pro. placed on aid

SKY PILOT (5.11c) Donner: Max Jones, Mark Hudon, 1977

SKY ROCKET (5.8) Lover's Leap: Steve Miller, Rick Sumner, 1978

SKYWALKER (5.10a) Donner: Bill Anderson, Gene Drake, 1981

SLASH, THE (5.8) P. Berry, R. Linnett, 1958

SLIP'N SLIDE (5.7) Echo Lakes: M. Franceshini and friend, 1973

SLIPSTREAM (5.11b) Donner: Max Jones, Gary Allen, 1976

SLITHERING SLIT (5.5) Echo Lakes: Bill Serniuk, solo

SLOT, THE (5.8) Pie Shop: unknown

SLOW DANCER (5.9) Phantom Spires: Eric Barrett and friends, 1978

SLOW HAND (5.10d) Donner: Eric Barrett and friends, 1981

SMOKESTACK, THE (5.6) Sugarloaf: unknown

SNAKE CHARMER (5.11b/c) Echo Lakes: Paul Crawford, Jay Smith, 1982

SPACE INVADERS (5.10a/b) Donner: Gene Drake, Rocko Rampino, 1981

SPACE TRUCKIN' (5.10a/b) Eagle Creek: Rick Cashner, Angie Morales, 1979

SPACEWALK (5.11d) Eagle Creek: Kevin Nelson, Bill Todd, 1973; FFA: Rick Cashner, Rick Sumner, 1979

SPLIT PEA (5.8) Donner: unknown

SQUEEZE AND WHEEZE (5.9) Echo Lakes: unknown

STAGE FRIGHT (5.9) Phantom Spires: Eric Barrett, Dave Stam, 1976

STEALIN' (5.10a A1) Phantom Spires: David Babich, Rick Spittler, Bob Conway; FFA: unknown

STEPPIN' STONE (5.11a) Phantom Spires: Eric Barrett, George Connor, Dave Stam, 1978; FFA: D. Richardson and friends, 1979

STONE (5.10a) Sugarloaf: Greg Dexter, Steve Miller, 1976

STONE COLD CRAZY (5.12c) Lover's Leap: Tony Yaniro, 1982

STONY END (5.11c) Lover's Leap: Tony Yaniro, Max Jones, 1982

STONY GOD (5.11d/5.12a) Lover's Leap: Tony Yaniro, 1982

STONY HIGHWAY (5.11c) Lover's Leap: Chris Clifford, 1984

STRAWBERRY OVERPASS (5.10b) Lover's Leap: Mark Nicholss, Brian Harrington, 1984

STRONTIUM 90 (5.8 tr) Eagle Creek: unknown

SUDDEN DEATH (5.8) Lover's Leap: (1st 2 pitches) Rick Cashner, Rick Sumner, 1979; (upper pitches) Richard Harrison, Jay Smith, 1977

SOUTH FACE Lizard Head (A3) Phantom Spires: Kevin Rivett, David Babich, 1978

SUMMER BREEZE (5.8) Echo Lakes: Mike Corbett, Bill Serniuk, 1979

SUPER SLAB (5.10a) Donner: Max Jones, Gary Allen, 1977

SURREALISTIC DIRECT (5.10a-5.10c) Lover's Leap: Jeff Lowe, J. Vives, 1969

SURREALISTIC PILLAR (5.7) Lover's Leap: K. Edsburg, M. Edsburg, J. Sublette, 1963

TALKING HEADS (5.11a) Phantom Spires: Jay Smith, Paul Crawford, 1982

TAPESTRY (5.10b) Sugarloaf: Rick Sumner, Bill Todd, 1977

TAURUS (5.11b) Sugarloaf: Mark Hudon, Max Jones, 1977

T- BONE (5.10d) Phantom Spires: Paul Crawford, Jay Smith, Lanny Johnson, Mark Hudon, 1984

TEACHER'S PET (5.10b) Donner: John Hoffman, 1975

TEEANAGE WASTELAND (5.10b) Pie Shop: Paul Crawford, Eric Alexander, 1979

TELEGRAPH (5.8) Donner: unknown

THING, THE (5.10d) Donner: Max Jones, 1978

THIRD STONE FROM THE SUN (5.10c) Lover's Leap: Richard Harrison, Steve Miller, Jay Smith, 1977

THRUST IS A MUST (5.10d) Eagle Creek: D. Grossman, Rick Van Horn, 1980

TIC-TIC-TIC (5.11a) Lover's Leap: Ed Drummond

TILT (5.10a) Donner: Gary Allen, Max Jones, 1977

TI-SA-ACK (5.10d tr) Eagle Creek: unknown

TIPTOE (5.10a) Donner: unknown

TM'S DEVIATION (5.9) Sugarloaf: TM Herbert, Bruce Cooke, 1968

TOMBSTONE TERROR (5.10c) Lover's Leap: Gary Anderson, Steve Miller, Jay Smith, Rick Sumner, 1976

TOUCH AND GO (5.9) Donner: Kim Schmitz, Norm Simmons, 1971

TRAVELER BUTTRESS (5.9) Lover's Leap: (below Main Ledge) Steve Roper, Steve Thompson, Gordon Webster, 1966; (above Main Ledge) unknown; FFA: Dick Long, Al Steck, 1965

TRUE GRIP (5.10b) Pie Shop: Paul Crawford, P. Steiner, 1975

TRUMPLED UNDER FOOT (5.10a) Sugarloaf: Paul Crawford and friends, 1978

TURNING POINT (5.10b) Phantom Spires: Don Spittler, David Babich, 1976; FFA: Eric Barrett, George Connor, 1978

TYRO'S TESTPIECE (5.5) Phantom Spires: unknown

UNDERCLING (5.8) Sugarloaf: unknown

UNDER THE BIG TOP (5.10d) Lover's Leap: Karl McConachie, Jay Smith, 1981

UNNAMED (5.7 A2) Phantom Spires: unknown

UP FOR GRABS (5.8) Phantom Spires: David Babich, Eric Barrett, 1978

UP FROM THE SKIES (5.10d) Lover's Leap: Paul Crawford, Paul Obanheim, Jay Smith, 1982

VANSIHING POINT (5.10a/b) Lover's Leap: Gene Drake, Jim Orey, 1972

VINTAGE 85 (5.9 tr) Eagle Creek: unknown

VOYEUR (5.9) Donner: Gary Allen, Max Jones, 1977

VULTURE, THE (5.10a) Eagle Creek: Jay Smith, Paul Crawford, Paul Obanheim, 1985

WALLFLOWER (5.10a-5.10c) Lover's Leap: Paul Crawford, Jay Smith, Bill Todd, 1976

WALRUS, THE (5.8 A3) Pie Shop: Bill Todd, 1976

WAVE RIDER (5.8) Lover's Leap: Gene Drake, Jim Hicks, 1970

WELCOME TO MY NIGHTMARE (5.11b) Donner: Max Jones, John Hoffman, 1979

WELL DONE (5.11d) Phantom Spires: Paul Crawford, Karl Mc-Conachie, 1984

WEST CHIMNEY (5.8) Sugarloaf: Warren Harding, John Ohrenschall, 1954

WEST WALL (5.8) Lover's Leap: K. Edsburg, A. McLane, 1965

WET DREAMS (5.11a) Phantom Spires: Krista Smith, Tom Smith, 1984

WE'VE CREATED A MONSTER (5.11b) Echo Lakes: Bob Albonico, Bret Alexander, Mark Stumpf, 1985

WILD TURKEY (5.8) Lover's Leap: Richard Harrison, Jay Smith, 1977

WIND (5.10b) Pie Shop: Paul Crawford, 1978

WIND TREE (5.9) Eagle Creek: Kevin Nelson, Bill Todd, 1974

WIPEOUT (5.11a) Pie Shop: Bill Todd, 1976

WOLF CRACK (5.12 tr) Donner: unknown

YODELLER (5.9) Echo Lakes: Mike Corbett, Bill Serniuk, Charlene Serniuk, 1979

ZIG ZAG FINISH (5.10a) Pie Shop: Paul Crawford, 1978

ZOO TRAMP (5.7-5.9) Phantom Spires: Kevin Rivett, David Babich, 1976

ROUTE INDEX